D0211195

THRILLING SCENES
AMONG THE INDIANS

CUSTER'S LAST RALLY.

THRILLING SCENES

AMONG THE INDIANS.

WITH A GRAPHIC DESCRIPTION OF

CUSTER'S LAST FIGHT WITH SITTING BULL.

BY

T. M. NEWSON.

Author of "LIFE IN THE BLACK HILLS," "INDIAN LEGENDS," Etc.

ILLUSTRATED.

1994

A Platinum Press Book

This special reprint edition originally published
in 1884 is now republished by:

Longmeadow Press
201 High Ridge Road
Stamford, CT 06904

in association with

Platinum Press Inc.
311 Crossways Park Drive
Woodbury, NY 11797

ISBN 0-681-00759-1

0987654321

Printed in the USA

Library of Congress Cataloging-in-Publication Data

Newson, T. M. (Thomas McLean), 1827-1893.
Thrilling scenes among the Indians / by T. M. Newson.
p. cm.
Originally published : Chicago : Belford, Clark & Co., 1888.
"A Platinum Press book."
ISBN 0-681-00759-1
1. Indians of North America — West (U.S.) — History. 2. Little Big Horn, Battle of the, 1876. I. Title.
E78.W5N48 1994
973.8'2 — dc20 94-11835
CIP

CONTENTS.

Mis-se-jar-ga; or, the Angel Guide................ 7
Indian Treachery; or a Run for Life.............. 14
Marriage and Death of Minnehaha................ 24
Birth Place of Minnehaha........................ 28
Indian Diplomacy................................ 30
Minnetooka; an Indian Legend................... 33
Thrilling Scenes Among the Indians.............. 45
Wenona; Maiden Rock............................ 55
Lake Pepin and Scenery......................... 59
Kis-se-me-pa and Kar-go-ga...................... 62
The Skulking Dog............................... 65
Pick-a-wa-ka and El-mo-na...................... 71
Memory of a Noted Chippewa Chief............... 75
He-le-o-pa and Nim-pe-wa-pa.................... 78
The Mississippi River; its Scenery.............. 83
The Battle for the Apron........................ 87
A White Indian Queen........................... 92
An Indian's Theory of the Celestial Bodies........ 93
The Inner Life of the Indian.................... 98
An-pe-tu-sa-pa; Legend of St. Anthony Falls...... 106
My Last Night in a Sioux Indian Camp........... 111
Peculiar Indian Traditions...................... 118
The Game of Ball—a Thrilling Scene............. 128
Pa-ha Wa-kan; or, the Sacred Descent............ 135
Old Bets; Romance of Early Life................ 141
Wa-zi-ya, and the Enchanted Knife............... 145
Opinions, Beliefs and Customs of the Indians...... 149

The Last Man—Strange Beliefs.................... 153
General George A. Custer.......................... 172
Sitting Bull, or Ta-tou-ka-i-y-a-tou-ka............. 178
The Last Great Indian Battle........................ 184
Sitting Bull's First Visit to Civilization............ 192
An Interesting Trip.................................. 201
A Genuine Scare...................................... 208
Fort Snelling 213
Indian Speeches and Indian Council 215
Early Missionary Efforts 221
Indian Poetry.
He Will Come... 236
Come Again 236
The Giant's Dance 237
Never, Never... 237
Grandfather 238
To the Spirit-land 238

PREFACE.

MOST of the scenes described, and nearly all the incidents narrated, in the pages of this book, were a part of my own personal experience of a residence of some thirty years on the frontier, and for which I can vouch as true, except, perhaps, the incidents of the last great battle of the lamented Custer with Sitting Bull, and for these I am indebted to one who was early on the ground after the conflict, and who has obtained from the Indians themselves what I deem to be a very accurate picture of the terrible struggle between the contending forces.

Of the various traditions which are woven in among the other articles, I can only say, in the language of Longfellow:

> "Should you ask where Na-wa-da-ha
> Found these songs, so wild and wayward,—
> Found these legends and traditions,—
> I should answer, I should tell tell you,
> In the bird's nests of the forest,
> In the lodges of the beaver,
> In the hoof-prints of the bison,
> In the eyrie of the eagle,
> Here Na-wa-da-ha found these legends."

The object of this work is to group together some of the traditions of the past and many of the characteristics of the Indians of the Northwest, and to so weave in romance and history as to form interesting reading matter for the general public. Several of the legends and articles now published have already appeared in print, and as they were then received with much cordiality, exhausting the various editions rapidly, the author feels warranted in the belief that the present volume will be favorably received by a discriminating public. All the habits, customs, beliefs, and puculiarities of the Indians can be relied upon as correct.

THE AUTHOR.

SAINT PAUL, Minn., 1884.

MIS-SE-JAR-GA;

OR, THE ANGEL GUIDE.

"WELL," I asked of an old Indian of nearly one hundred winters, who sat over a camp fire, smoking his well-worn pipe, "What legend do you know of a body of water recognized by the white man as Lake of the Loons?" He gave a grunt, emptied the ashes from his pipe, refilled it with kinnikinick, puffed away for a few moments, and then said:

"Many moons long since gone, when my hair was black and my face was smooth, away off to the east, where the bright spirit—the sun—rises and washes its face in the morning dews, dwelt my forefathers, and the friends of my youth. Just on the border of our reservation settled a paleface and his family, which at first made our hearts bad, but they were so good and so kind that we came to esteem them, and they lived among us respected. His family consisted of three boys, and a golden-haired girl of five summers. This child was as fair as Minnehaha, beautiful as sunset, happy as a bird, gentle as a lamb, sweet as the Great Spirit. Her winning ways, her golden, curly hair, her great blue eyes, her innocent prattle, her confidence in the red man, as she climbed on his knee and toyed with his long black hair—the contrast between the sweet lily face and the tawny complexion of our tribe, won for her the name of Mis-se-jar-ga, or the angel guide."

The old Indian paused, dropped his head upon his

breast; was silent for a moment, when, with another puff from his pipe, he proceeded with his story.

"White mother loved child; white man loved child. One Indian loved child better than white man. Child good. Child angel. Heap big heart for Mis-se-jar-ga."

A deep, guttural sound escaped from the old Indian, as he paused again and gazed intently into the fire, and he was only aroused from his reverie by my asking him: "Lelia cooler, good friend, what then?"

"Indian steals up close to white man's wigwam. Night has covered the beautiful face with darkness; Mis-se-jar-ga sleeps, but Indian loved Mis-se-jar-ga. He takes her up like a pure snow-flake, wraps her in his blanket, and before she is conscious, glides out into the forest, and ere the morning dawns, is a day's travel towards the west. Moons come and go, but no Mis-se-jar-ga. Family mourn, but no Mis-se-jar-ga. Mother dies from grief, but no Mis-se-jar-ga. Brothers hunt the woods for the bones of their beautiful sister, but no Mis-se-jar-ga. No angel guide comes to comfort the weary heart of the white father. Mis-se-jar-ga is gone forever toward the setting sun.

"Harry was the youngest brother of Mis-se-jar-ga. Many, many, more moons had passed, since the boy had grown to manhood. The memory of his golden-haired sister still dwelt in his heart. He had suspicions that she still lived. The father had crossed the river of death and had joined the mother in the spirit land, and the brothers, disposing of their farm, had gone back to their friends in the east. Harry lived only for one end—one aim—one purpose—the restoration of his sister."

Again the Indian dropped his head on his breast and

was silent. I let him remain so, when rousing up, he continued:

"Harry had come to know the Indian language, the Indian costumes, the Indian mode of living, and bidding good-bye to the old homestead, equipped as a trapper, he set out for the Mississippi river, where he had good reason to believe his sister had been carried."

I here interrupt the story of the Indian to explain to the reader, that the place where Harry's father had opened his farm, was in the extreme eastern portion of Wisconsin, where, at that time, no white man but he had ever dared to venture. The country was wholly inhabited by the children of the forest, who since then have been moving rapidly westward, and for hundreds of miles where they used to roam, are now cities and cultivated farms. One can form a vivid conception of how difficult it must have been for Harry to traverse this wide extent of country, looking for his long-lost sister.

The Indian resumed his narrative.

"Trapping along the streams, hunting game in the woods, sleeping upon the ground, or occasionally enjoying the hospitality of an Indian tepee. Harry traveled continually, buoyed up with the hope of meeting the blue-eyed Mis-se-jar-ga, whose dear little features haunted him night and day. He had forgotten that ten years had elapsed since her abduction—he had forgotten that the child had bloomed into the young girl—had forgotten that her mode of life had changed her—had forgotten that the clear complexion had merged into the copper-colored tint of the Indian maiden. All he saw, all he dreamed of, all he thought of, was the golden-haired child of his boyhood.

"When within about two days' travel of the Mississippi river, Harry drew his rifle and fired at a deer as it bounded past him. Instantly he heard wild warwhoops, and saw thirteen Indians bearing down upon him, with uplifted knives and tomahawks. In vain he assured them he was their friend—in vain he talked to them in their native tongue; but a white man had never been seen in their country before; to them he must be a spy, an enemy, so finding it useless to make a fight, he threw down his gun and surrendered. The Indians drew near, seized his weapon, his knife, his hunter's dress, and binding his hands behind him, ordered him to follow them. They crossed the Mississippi and continued on, until they came to a lake, about whose shores were heavy trees, and here they were met by other Indians who came to see the prisoner. This was their camping ground, their home. Harry was conducted to a small birch-bark tepee, somewhat separated from the rest, and after his arms were more securely bound, and his feet firmly fastened, he was left alone with only one Indian to guard the door."

The old Indian turned his head quickly, seized his rifle as it were by intuition, crouched down upon the ground, and after a moment or two relaxed into his usual composure, and continued his story.

"That night the Indians gathered in a council of death, near where lay the white man, listening and understanding all they said. The old braves advocated burning at the stake, with a war-dance. The paleface had invaded their country; he came to do them harm; he had a bad spirit, so sentence of death was passed upon him, to be executed in two days. The council broke up with a wild, weird, thrilling death song, which fell upon the ears of Harry like leaden bullets.

"Morning dawned, and with it no hope for the condemned man! Harry knew enough of Indian character to realize that his doom was sealed, so he begged as a last boon that he might be permitted to stroll along the shores of the lake and commune with nature before death ended his career. Oh, if he could see that sister once more before he died; if he could but know that she still lived, it would enable him to endure the terrible end which he knew must come. Some distance below the lodge where he had been imprisoned, and upon the borders of the lake, partially hidden by beautiful trees and creeping vines, was another tepee; and as the prisoner walked along the shore natural curiosity induced the Indian women to gaze upon him. Harry looked up, caught the glance of a girl of fifteen years, with Indian complexion, Indian dress, Indian timidity, but *with golden, curly hair and blue eyes!* Could it be possible! Was that his sister? His head grew dizzy; he tottered, fainted and fell. When he came to himself, two Indians and several squaws were bending over him, and among them the young maiden whose image had frozen his heart. He spoke to her in English, she heeded him not; he spoke to her in Indian, telling her she must be his sister,—he alluded to her hair, her eyes, so different from the Indian, but her memory was blank; he could make no impression. He asked permission to lift the scarf that encircled her neck; beneath it was pure white. He *knew* it was his sister, but how could he make her realize it? During this interview the Indians gazed with astonishment and awe upon the scene! They began to get uneasy. The Indian maiden herself was withdrawing to her tepee, when Harry, desperate with his desire to have her recognize him, once more began talking with her in Indian. He spoke of her childhood; her brothers, her parents, her abduction; but it brought no light to the memory of the poor girl. Finally he alluded to the name of Harry, to her early play ground, her baking cakes in the sand, her romping with her little brother; and then, in an instant, came back the light of other days. She approached him; asked him to repeat the name of Harry; asked him to tell her more about the sand cakes, and then, all of a sudden, uttered a piercing scream, fell to the earth, and was carried to her tepee, while Harry was conducted back to his prison house, amid great confusion in the camp.

"That night there was another council, and in the midst of it stood the Indian girl, her blue eyes flashing and her golden curls floating down her back. It was Mis-se-jar-ga, the angel guide, whose influence with the tribe was unbounded. She plead for the life of the paleface. It might be her brother, it might not be; but why take the life of the white man, who had done them no harm? why incur the ill will of the Great Spirit, in doing a great wrong? Her efforts were endorsed by a young and handsome brave, in an eloquent plea, not so much for the white man, as for the wishes of the Indian maiden, and before the council adjourned, the savages had relented, the death sentence had been changed to liberty, and that night Harry walked among the red men, a happy man, for he had gained his life and found his long-lost sister.

"That memorable spot," said the old Indian, pointing across the lake, "where Mis-se-jar-ga spent her early childhood—where she was recognized by her brother, and where she left the Indian camp forever to dwell among her own people, is over there, yonder, in that quiet little dell, where the tall trees sing of her beauty and of her innocence, and the waves of the lake bewail the absence of the ANGEL GUIDE.

INDIAN TREACHERY.

A RUN FOR LIFE.

NINETEEN years ago, while on my way from Vermilion lake, near the British line, I found that the spring floods had carried away all the bridges, had stopped the stages, indeed, had interrupted all travel to such an extent that pedestrians were obliged to either walk through water and mud some thirty or forty miles per day—as the stage stations were then about this distance apart on the traveled road—or lay up at one of the "inns" along the line. I, with my companion, a short, duck-legged chap, by the name of Camp, who had come with me from Vermilion, decided, per force of necessity, to stop at a place called "Deer Creek;" so "housing in," we adapted ourselves to circumstances, and becoming more fully acquainted with the landlord and his wife, soon whiled away the time in real primitive, frontier style. The rain out doors beat against the window panes, it leaked through the roof, it whipped in under the door; the swollen stream, after which the place took its name, roared and foamed, and tossed close by the little house in which we were huddled; the good dame had fried her salt pork and slap-jacks, and was just on the point of calling us to dinner, when two weary travelers sprung in the door and dripping with water, tired with walking, exhausted with hunger, stood before us, objects of our deepest commiseration. Of course they were soon made comfortable, supplied with food, and in a short time we found ourselves quite good friends, for nothing binds men together more closely or cements stronger friendships, than adversity itself, and as we were all at the mercy of the good people of "Deer Creek" and the raging storm without, we became particularly interested in each other and philosophers at large.

One of these men was small and wiry, the other had a large, heavy frame, and a swarthy complexion. About an hour after dinner the small man drew me aside, and said confidentially—"You see my companion?" I answered, "I did." "Well," he remarked, "he is an Indian, possessed of a great secret, and as I know you are interested in what I am about to say, I will communicate something to you of great importance, but I want it understood as strictly confidential," to which of course I assented. "Well, then," said my companion, "that Indian, disguised in a white man's dress, under which is his own garb, knows where there is a large and rich deposit of metal. You see those earrings, those finger rings and that pipe, all of solid silver? Well, he cut that metal right out of the rock, and he knows just where it is!" "Is that so?" I asked. "Yes," said the small, wiry man, "and what is more, I will get him to go with you and show you where it is." I said to Camp, "I'm off in the morning up country, on an important errand; will you go?" To which he replied, "Yes." So, soon after this, matters were arranged with the Indian, whereby I was to pay him $50 when he had shown me the place from whence the silver in his possession had been obtained, and we concluded to commence our journey the next day. Camp, the Indian and myself started out on foot, and after traveling for nearly three days, came to the spot where the vein was said to be located, but here the Indian halted, under a superstition, no doubt, of his race, that if he told a white man where the "shoon-e-ar," or money was, that a spirit would kill him, so he prevaricated, stumbled, paused, and finally claimed that the water was too high; he could not find the place, etc., etc. Disgusted, Camp, myself and my "cowin nisisshin," not good guide, set out to the nearest house, knowing full well that we must either make it, or remain all night in the woods. Camp's little duck legs were put to their utmost capacity, but he kept close on to my heels in a state of perspiration, as we tripped through a dense woods, and after a walk of fifteen miles, emerged into an opening, on the stage-traveled road, where was an old claim shanty, occupied by one O'Rally, a clever Irishman, who, seeing our chilled and tired condition, set before us a hot whisky punch, and in a short time we were in a placid and pleasant state of mind. During our trip through the woods, I had observed that my Indian guide evidently intended to detain us in the forest until after dark, and this, with some other peculiar actions upon his part, especially after O'Rally had given him some "Scoot-ta-wa-boo," or whisky, to drink, led me to suspect that the fellow was contemplating mischief, but I said nothing to Camp. While in this state of mind, and undecided whether I would go on ten miles further that evening to catch the stage in the morning, or remain over where we were, I observed peeping into the window, a strange, hideous Indian face, black, with angry eyes, high cheek bones, a large, firmly set mouth, and huge jaws. He gazed at me so ferociously that I actually cowered under his penetrating glare. And then I observed that the other Indian who had been with us was talking with him, and both were armed with knives, tomahawks, etc.,—my guide having doffed his white man's dress for that of his own—and what made matters still more serious, was the fact that they were both under the influence of whisky. I had seen a great deal of Indian character under various phases, but I had never before seen a savage that I positively feared so much as that black, devilish face and those glaring eyes, that ever and anon peered in through the window upon me.

Fifteen minutes had passed and I had seen no Indians. Well, I thought to myself, they have gone home. I went out of the house and looked round—nobody to be seen. It was getting towards sun-down. Could we make the next station before dark? It was a very desolate and dangerous road, but as my especial fear was removed in the non-appearance of the Indians, I decided to go on; so I said to Camp, "We will make for the next station. As those devilish Indians have gone, I have no fear, and we can foot it lively." It had never entered Camp's head that the Indians might attack and kill us on the road, for if he had had the least suspicion in this direction, he would not have budged an inch. Something in my look, however, must have aroused his suspicion, for he came close to me, and looking piteously into my face, asked—"Do you think there is any danger on the road?" "Oh, no," I replied. I didn't like that Indian with a dark face, but I guess we are now clear of them, and we better go on." "You know we are not armed," said Camp. "Yes, I know, but you have that old ax; better take it along with you."

Bidding good-bye to our friend, we started out on a

brisk walk just as the sun was climbing down the mountains, and winding around a curve, struck into a narrow road that lay at the foot of high hills on the right, and gorges eight hundred feet deep on the left. The rocky cliffs frowned down upon us while the dark chasms below sent back dull, heavy thug sounds, as we rolled stones over the precipice and heard them gurgle in the bottom below. Just ahead of us was a descent in the road, and we could see a little brook bubbling over the rocks and making its way down, down, down, amid a dark sea of foliage, one thousand feet below, and as we drew nearer we observed that the ravine through which this stream ran, was spanned by a crude, narrow bridge, and to my utmost horror, on this bridge, in a partial state of intoxication, sat the two identical Indians I so much feared. They were talking humorously with themselves; swaying to and fro, and did not notice us until we were close upon them, when they broke out in their Indian dialect: "Booshu, neches! Kersmokerman ogamar, scoot-ta-wa-boo, nisisshin," which means in English—"How do you do, friends! White man chief, whisky is good."

At the same time, the ugly, dark-faced Indian got up, and approaching me, sought by force to place me on the bridge between the two. I took in the whole situation at a glance, for once in their clutches, I knew a knife would soon penetrate my heart, and my body would go rolling down the deep abyss, while poor Camp would soon after suffer the same fate; so, straightening myself up and assuming an air of defiance, I pushed back the advancing Indian, and uttered in a loud voice, "Cowin nisisshin," not good. "Cowin!" I won't drink. Their hilarity deepened into an ugly scowl.

They had been foiled. They were armed with knives and tomahawks; I had nothing but a pen-knife, and Camp had an old ax, but we conveyed the impression that I had a revolver, which no doubt had much to do in keeping them at bay. Finding that I would not drink, that I was sullen and still, they passed the bottle to each other, and then muttering to themselves, marched on ahead of us.

"Camp," I said, as he crept close to my side, "I am afraid we are going to have trouble with those Indians." "Oh! my God!" said Camp, "do you think they will kill us? Oh, my God, my God!" "Well, Camp, their motives are bad, and the only way we can save our lives is by boldness and strategy. If they knew I was unarmed, they would kill us in a minute. Now do just as I tell you, or your life won't be worth ten cents." "Oh, don't talk so; for God's sake don't talk so; I'm trembling all over! What a terrible place to be in on this road! Look into that dark valley below! If my body should go down there, my family would never find the remains of poor Camp. What a fool to come out here to this horrible place. But do you really think they will attack us?" "Listen. A certain distance ahead, they will sit down and await our coming, and then they will try to induce me to drink again. One of the Indians, under a pretext of lightening your burden, will seek to get your ax, but don't you let it go out of your hand at the peril of your life. If it become necessary, swing it and strike that dark visaged Indian dead; we can manage the other. They are getting drunker and drunker, and of course more ferocious. It is darkening into twilight, and I must confess the outlook is very serious." Camp's little duck-legs made several circles for a few minutes, while he ejaculated—"oh! oh! oh!" and then looking more like a dead man than a live one, promised faithfully to do as I bid him, and we jogged on.

True enough, a little way ahead of us, there sat the Indians awaiting our coming, and as we approached them, one offered me the bottle of whisky, and the other sought to take from Camp his ax. He had nearly succeeded, when Camp, turning upon his heel, swung the ax high in the air, and it came within an inch of the head of the ugly savage, which movement I immediately seconded by stepping up to Mr. Indian, and putting my fist into his face, ordered him to let that man alone. Our actions had the desired effect, but we could plainly see that the infuriated beasts, urged on by whisky, were getting madder and madder, and that it needed strategy as well as bravery to carry our point. We had now made at least about eight miles, and had two more to make before we reached Damphier's, the station from which the stage left in the morning. This the Indians were aware of as well as ourselves, and if they intended to bag their game, they knew and we knew, they had got to do it soon. If treachery was their point, I intended to meet them on that ground, so softening my ways, I took the bottle from my dusky friends and with a loud "Ho!" drank, that is, I let most of the fluid slip down under my coat, instead of into my throat, but it appeased their increasing hatred and I had gained the point I desired to utilize in our next heat, which I knew would be the most exciting, if not the fatal one in our career. The Indians, apparently, overjoyed at my friendship—which I knew was only a feint—brandished their knives high in the air, glared out into the increasing darkness, and hardly able to stand up, commenced their terrible war-dance, yelling, as only Indians can yell, when on the scent of blood. Poor Camp stood by trembling like an aspen leaf, when we both started to move along, but the Indians glided in ahead of us, and in an excited manner, soon gained an advance.

"Camp, you see that hill ahead of us?" "Yes." "Well, just over it is Damphier's. We have got to make that point on the virtue of our limbs, or we shall never reach civilization!" "Oh, my God! my God," exclaimed Camp. "You know I can't run; I am a dead man; those devils will get me sure." "Well, it is our only course. It is a run for life, so make up your mind to get over that ground just as fast as the Lord will let you." Camp gave a low groan. "When we come up to the Indians again, I will affect to drink with them and get them thoroughly engaged in narrating some of their great deeds of valor, and on a given signal you walk ahead unobserved, and on another signal, throw aside your ax, take your boots in your hands, or throw them away, and make for the station house with all the power you possess. I will catch up with you, and we may yet be saved." We soon came up to where the Indians were sitting, and I went in strong with them on drinking, being careful to let the fiery stuff eat the lining of my coat rather than the lining of my throat. They were infuriated drunk, ready for any dark deed, with courage strong enough to kill a dozen white men, but I adroitly drew them into a discussion as to the relative merits of their own deeds; gave the signals to Camp; moved away from them quietly, and in the next five minutes Camp's short, banty legs were cutting amusing figures on the brow of the hill, while my own limbs were making music close behind him. "Go it, Camp!" I cried, and Camp was going it—no hat—no boots—no coat. Just before I reached the top of the hill, I looked back, and found that the Indians had discovered our flight, and were coming for us in the most horrible manner, wild with whisky, reeking with revenge for their disappointment, cutting the air with their knives and tomahawks, screaming, running, howling—presenting one of the most revolting scenes I had ever witnessed. I had caught up with Camp, and we were neck and neck. "There's the house," I exclaimed, "hold out a little longer," and away we ran, the Indians gaining upon us every minute. We could almost feel their hot breath, and in imagination see the descending tomahawk entering our skulls, when Camp went head foremost into Damphier's door, and in an instant it was fastened by a heavy wooden bar, and the next moment our frantic foes gave a bang—they were just behind us, but too late! Camp went turning over and over on the floor, trying to gain his breath, claiming he was dying, while Damphier sent his family into the log part of the building, and with his double-barreled gun made his appearance for the fight. Again came bang against the door! again I saw those glittering eyes—again another bang, bang, when Damphier told them, through the window, that just one more bang would cost them their lives, and after skulking about for several hours, trying the windows and the doors, all was still. Camp got up and became composed. The family gathered together, but there was no sleep that night—we were all on watch until the gray of the morning, and I was heartily glad when the stage took us whirling away from this dreadful spot.

A few weeks 'ater I learned that it was the intention of these Indians to have killed us on the road, to have robbed me, as it was supposed by them I had money on my person, and from all I could gather, the small wiry man who gave me the first information of the big Indian at " Deer Creek," was the original instigator in the whole plot.

I have a vivid recollection of two things, viz: the glaring eyes of that horrible Indian, and the little duck legs of Camp as he peeled it over the hill, in A RUN FOR DEAR LIFE.

MARRIAGE AND DEATH OF MINNE-HAHA.

MINNE (WATER) HA! HA! (LAUGHING)—LAUGHING WATER.

THE poet Longfellow has made memorable in song, Minne-ha-ha, or Laughing Water, a beautiful little cascade that goes dancing over a precipice, and then the joyous brook from whence it comes, gurgles its way onward to the Mississippi river. Previous to forming the cascade, Minnehaha creek receives its life from, and is connected with, a lake, and thus meandering through forest and glen, and over pebbly shores and through cultivated farms, it at last, like a young girl, with wild, flowing locks and sparkling eyes, leaps over the broken rocks and scatters pearls in the dark chasm below.

The poet has pictured Hiawatha as great in his own estimation, and who, after having achieved greatness in the eyes of others, conceived the idea of uniting the antagonistic Indian elements of two ferocious tribes, by he, a Chippewa, marrying Minnehaha, a Dacotah maiden, with whom he is really in love. His soliloquy on marriage is beautiful. He says:

> "As unto the bow the cord is,
> So unto man is woman;
> Though she bends him, she obeys him,
> Though she draws him, yet she follows—
> Useless each without the other."

Having settled this point in his own mind, he persists in his determination to unite himself to a woman of a different tribe, and in response to old No-ko-mis, who objects to his union, he replies :

> " In the land of the Dacotahs
> Lives the arrow-maker's daughter,
> Minnehaha, Laughing Water,
> Handsomest of all the women.
> I will bring her to your wigwam,
> She shall run upon your errands,
> Be your starlight, moonlight, firelight,
> Be the sunshine of your people."

No-ko-mis rejoins :

> " Very fierce are the Dacotahs;
> There are feuds yet unforgotten,
> Wounds that ache and still may open."

To which Hiawatha answers :

> " For that reason, if no other,
> Would I wed the fair Dacotah,
> That our tribes might be united,
> That old feuds might be forgotten,
> And old wounds be healed forever."

With this determination he sets off to the land of his lady-love, who years ago he met and admired, and after various feats of valor, among which was the killing of a deer, and " at each stride a mile he measured," he arrives at the coveted spot. I leave Longfellow to tell the balance of the story in his own inimitable style :

> " At the door-way of his wigwam
> Sat the ancient arrow-maker,
> In the land of the Dacotahs,
> Making arrow-heads of jasper,
> Arrow-heads of chalcedony.
> At his side, in all her beauty,
> Sits his daughter, Laughing Water,
> Plaiting mats of flags and rushes;
> Of the past the old man's thoughts were,
> And the maiden's of the future.

She was thinking of a hunter,
From another tribe and country,
Young and tall and very handsome,
Who, one morning, in the spring-time,
Came to buy her father's arrows,
Sat and rested in the wigwam,
Lingered long about the doorway,
Looking back as he departed.
She had heard her father praise him,

Praise his courage and his wisdom;
Would he come again for arrows
To the Falls of Minnehaha?
On the mat her hands lay idle,
And her eyes were very dreamy.

Through their thoughts they heard a footstep,
Heard a rustling in the branches,
And with glowing cheeks and forehead,
With the deer upon his shoulders,
Suddenly from out the woodlands
Hiawatha stood before them.

Straight the ancient arrow-maker
Looked up gravely from his labor,
Laid aside the unfinished arrow,
Bade him enter at the doorway,
Saying, as he rose to meet him,
"Hiawatha, you are welcome!"

At the feet of Laughing Water
Hiawatha laid his burden,
Threw the red deer from his shoulders:
And the maiden looked up at him,
Looked up from her mat of rushes,
Said with gentle look and accent,
"You are welcome, Hiawatha!"

* * * * *

Listened while the guest was speaking,
Listened while her father answered,
But not once her lips she opened,
Not a single word she uttered.

Yet, as in a dream, she listened
To the words of Hiawatha,
As he talked of old No-ko-mis,
Who had nursed him in his childhood.
And of happiness and plenty
In the land of the Ojibways,
In the pleasant land and peaceful.

"After many years of warfare,
Many years of strife and bloodshed,
There is peace among the Ojibways,
And the tribe of the Dacotahs."
Thus continued Hiawatha,
And then added, speaking slowly:
"That this peace may last forever,
And our hands be clasped more closely,
And our hearts be more united,
Give me as my wife this maiden,
MINNEHAHA, Laughing Water,
Loveliest of Dacotah women!"

And the ancient arrow-maker
Paused a moment ere he answered,
Looked at Hiawatha proudly,
Finally looked at Laughing Water,
And made answer very gravely:
"Yes, if Minnehaha wishes;
Let your heart speak, Minnehaha!"

And the lovely Laughing Water
Seemed more lovely as she stood there,
Neither willing nor reluctant,
As she went to Hiawatha,
Softly took a seat beside him,
While she said, and blushed to say it,
"I will follow you, my husband!"

This was Hiawatha's wooing!
Thus it was he won the daughter
Of the ancient arrow-maker,
In the land of the Dacotahs.

From the wigwam he departed,
Leading with him Laughing Water;

Hand in hand they went together,
Through the woodland and the meadow;
Left the old man standing lonely
At the doorway of his wigwam,
Heard the Falls of Minnehaha
Calling to them from the distance,
Crying to them from afar off,
"Fare thee well, O Minnehaha!"

Time wanes and the famine appears. Hiawatha goes into the forest to hunt for food for his starving wife, but the deep snows prevent him from obtaining game. While in the woods, in imagination, he hears Minnehaha crying, "Hiawatha! Hiawatha!" and hastening home he enters his wigwam, to find his beautiful Laughing Water dead. And this legend, so finely told by Longfellow, has made immortal Minnehaha!

BIRTH-PLACE OF MINNEHAHA.

The Falls of Minnehaha are in Hennepin county, Minnesota. On the ground is a good hotel and places for rustic picnics. The cataract is about thirty feet wide in an ordinary stage of water, and leaps down into the ravine sixty feet. The water has a light, sparkling, foamy appearance, and after reaching the bottom, ripples along to the Mississippi river.

After entering the ground and reaching the ravine, just opposite, on the other side, can be seen the spot, dotted with trees, where once existed the wigwam of the old arrow-maker, and where was born and dwelt in peaceful loveliness, Minnehaha, or Laughing Water. The place then was more studded with nature's handiwork than now, and the quiet little home of the fair maiden nestled close to the merry rivulet that kept harmony with her own sweet voice in her songs of the forest. But what changes have taken place since then.

Gone are the Indians!—gone is the beautiful maiden!—gone is Hiawatha!—gone are many of the trees!—gone the deer! and in their places have come culture and civilization; and yet Minnehaha lives on, commemorating the memory of one made immortal by the magic pen of the poet, and the echoes from the past come back, ever singing, MINNEHAHA! MINNEHAHA!

INDIAN DIPLOMACY.

ADROITNESS OF AN INDIAN CHIEF.

THIRTY-TWO years ago, Govenor Ramsey, of Minnesota, was called upon to adjust serious difficulties which existed between the two powerful tribes of Indians existing in the then Territory of Minnesota, and to this end he called a council of the Sioux and Chippewa nations to meet at Fort Snelling, where troops and cannon could be made available in case of an outbreak. The council was to be held just outside of the walls of the fort, in the open space where the old Government stables used to stand, and on the open prairie between the garrison and the stable buildings. The tribes were on very good terms with the whites, but at deadly enmity with each other, to such an extent that almost daily murders occurred among them, and it needed the interposition of the strong arm of the Government to stay the treacherous knife and the fatal tomahawk; so in June, 1850, the council met at the place designated. Early in the day the Chippewas made their appearance, and took up their position, outside of the walls of the fort, rather enjoying the occasion as one of fun and frolic. At length the Sioux made their appearance on the brow of a hill across the St. Peter, now better known as the Minnesota river, and on they came, pell-mell, as though they intended to gobble up—Indian style—fort, troops, cannon, guns and their inveterate savage foe, the Chippewas. Rev. E. D. Neill, who was an eye witness to the scene, says:

"The few infantry present, on the approach of the Sioux, were extended in an open line, nearly from the fort to the stables, so as to form a separation between the Chippewas in their rear and the advancing band of the Sioux, numbering, perhaps, three hundred, a large portion on horseback, armed and painted, who by this time were rushing up on to the plateau, screaming and whooping horribly, themselves loaded with jingling arms and ornaments, and their horses with bells on, the whole of them galloping at full speed and making a feint as if they would pass around the stable, turn the right flank of the infantry and attack the Chippewas; but they were only showing off; they stood in fear of those ugly cannon that frowned down from the walls of the fort. The Sioux soon fell back and formed a line, discharging their pieces in a scattering fire as they did so. The Chippewas returned the salute; the guns from the fort responded, when a white flag appeared between the two opposite lines, and the two tribes stacked their arms. Then returning, the two lines advanced until they reached the file of infantry which separated them, when the chiefs and braves met at the centre between the lines, and, advancing, went through the ceremony of shaking hands. At a certain point in the council meeting it was observed that the Sioux had left en masse, and upon inquiry, it seems that their highnesses had taken offense at the presence of the ladies in council, and word came in that they thought they were to meet Chippewas in council, not women. HOLE-IN-THE-DAY, the noted chief, turned the matter to his own advantage, saying very politely, that he was happy to see so many sweet women there, and that they were all welcome with their angelic smiles to a seat on his side of the council. The ladies, however, when they heard what had occurred, chose to withdraw, the young Chippewa chief shaking each one cordially by the hand as they retired. The Sioux having returned, the Governor rebuked them sharply for their act of disrespect to the council, saying, that if they withdrew again in that manner, he would enforce the treaty of 1843. The two tribes finally agreed to be friendly, and the council adjourned, but the act of HOLE-IN-THE-DAY was the talk of the whites for years afterward, and is remembered very kindly even by the ladies of to-day, one of whom is the wife of ex-secretary of war, Ramsey, of Minnesota.

MIN-NE-TOO-KA.

A LEGEND OF M-DE-A-TON-KA.

WA-KAN—WAR-KA-NON—MAN-I-TOU—MIN-NE-TOO-KA.

IT was a beautiful day in June, 1854, when I arrived at Lake M-de-a-ton-ka, and taking a small and rudely constructed boat, was soon to a point midway of the lake, well known to the old settlers as the dividing line between the Sioux and Chippewa nations, where many a bloody battle had been fought, and where many a warrior had gone down to the sleep of death. I ascended gradually from the lake to a height of some thirty feet, winding over an Indian trail, through a mass of rich foliage, blooming flowers, creeping vines, singing birds, chirping squirrels, massive trees, cooling shades, changing scenery, until I reached the top, and there a grand sight met my view. Stretching off in the distance was the sparkling water, and from various knolls ascended the smoke of the wigwam, where the women were engaged in the sugar bush, while the men dotted the lake in their light canoes, in quest of game for their evening meal. The sun shone brightly, and a thousand diamonds seemed to glitter on the bosom of the fair lake, as the silvery waves rippled against the pebbly shore, and darted back again, like a beautiful maiden toying with her jewels. Here and there were bays and inlets and promontories; nooks and quiet, secluded points; yonder was a dark, forbidding spot, thickly studded with trees, and as I gazed upon it, I could see that it was the resting place of the dead, or the land of the supernatural, where the Man-i-tou and War-ka-non (Indian spirits) reveled in their nightly visits to their earthly friends. Just at the right of me, and near where I stood, ran a bubbling brook, now quietly nestling under the cover of brush and trees; now dashing and laughing over the impediments in its way; now romping gaily onward to the lake. At my back was a charming spot, overlooking the whole scene I have described, and in it, shut out from vulgar gaze by the thick foliage of the under brush, was an Indian tepee, with little, timid heads peeping out from under it, and a stalwart chief smoking his pipe near its entrance. As I approached, the chief arose, took his pipe from his mouth, greeted me cordially by a shake of the hand, and with a "How, cooler?"—how to do?—pointed to a log near him, where I soon was seated.

"Beautiful, lovely, charming spot," I exclaimed somewhat enthusiastically, to which the chief responded—"ho!" "Heap big amount of fish—heap big game," again I ventured to remark, to which came back again the inevitable "ho!" All was silent.

The reader must remember that the Indian can never be hurried, except in case of war or dinner. He has no particular pressing business—no notes to pay—no landlord to demand his rent—no butcher to poke a bill under his nose—no groceryman to stop his flour if pay don't come—no big parties to give in order to keep up appearances—no hired help to dog him about and bore him for services rendered—no fashionable society to cringe to—indeed, no particular labor, for the squaws perform the menial duties of the household, so he is really independent. If he is hungry, he knows where the game is, and a few hours' hunt will suffice to replenish the larder, at least until the next day. Beside, he takes no thought for the morrow, as he knows that if in want the tribe must share with him. Hence he is lymphatic, not nervous; stoical, not gushing; cool, not ardent; taking his own time—moving in his own way.

I sat at least ten minutes in silence, smoking the pipe which the old chief alternately passed to me, when I broke the stillness by requesting him to tell me something of the early history of the lake, what legend, if any, pertained to it, what battles had been fought, what superstitions existed, etc., etc., to which he gave only a guttural response of "ho," coolly refilled his pipe, peered out into the sunlight, gave several rapid puffs, to be sure that the kinnikinick was well lighted, and then said:

INDIAN LEGEND.

Many springs, and many moons, and many leaves of the forest, and many kinsmen of Ink-pa-go-da have come and gone, since the Chippewas stealthily crept down upon a band of Sioux, numbering thirty, near where we now sit, and in a moment, all unconscious to our brave warriors, desolated our hunting ground with the blood of the slain. The slaughter was indiscriminate, men, women and children; but one beautiful maiden was left, and she, it seems, was hidden by a Chippewa lover, who, when the fatal tomahawk was about to descend, arrested the blow, seized her around the waist, and with the agility of a panther, placed her safely in a secluded spot, where, when the battle was over, he intended to return and claim her as his own. Days passed, but no Indian was visible. Hunger drove the maiden from her seclusion, to pick berries to sustain life, but while in the act, she was met by a Sioux Indian chief and the Chippewa warrior who had saved her from death. Terribly frightened, she fled back to her place of safety, but to her great astonishment the Indians glided along with her, so that when she had reached the spot from whence she came, they were there also. The heart-rending memory of the death of her whole band; the fear of the Chippewa, which she did not at first recognize, caused her to crouch down in one corner of her hiding place and call upon Man-i-tou, the great spirit of scalps, to protect her in this, her hour of dreadful distress. To her astonishment, when she looked up, she beheld a kindly smile upon the chief's face, but a spirit of sadness brooded over the young Chippewa brave.

"Min-ne-too-ka," said the chief, "fear not. I am sent by Man-i-tou to aid you. You see me; you hear me speak, and yet you cannot touch me. I have come from the happy hunting ground, and with me is War-ka-non, who loves you. He loved you when he saved your life. He loved you when in crossing the lake he lost his own; he loves you as a spirit yet, and comes back to minister to your comfort."

Min-ne-too-ka did not dare to stir. She crept still closer to her hiding place. Her heart beat violently and she trembled.

"Fear not, Min-ne-too-ka," said War-ka-non, in a gentle and sweet voice. My people panted for the blood of the Sioux, and oh, the horrors of that night. I could not see you stricken down with the rest, and so I saved your life in hopes of a union on earth, but I am now beyond the mere materiality of the world. I walk in the happy hunting ground, but I am not happy because you are not there."

"Can it be possible," asked Min-ne-too-ka, "that these forms that I see before me are mere shadows of what they once were?"

"No," said War-ka-non, "we are the living realities of material men—the real men themselves."

"Tell me," said the maiden, as she gained confidence and drew near the two Indians, "if you be what you purport to be—spirits—if you come from that unseen land, tell me, where are my father, my mother, my sisters and my brothers?"

"They are all there, Min-ne-too-ka," replied War-ka-non. With the red wand they passed the bad spirits, with the blue wand they passed the tempting spirits, with the white wand they passed into the beginning of a higher life."

"Strange," said Min-ne-too-ka, "let me touch you!"

"No," said the chief and his companion, "that would not do, because you would dissolve our materiality, without which you could not see us. We put on this material dress in order to make ourselves known. When we pass from you, we become invisible to earthly eyes, but visible to spiritual eyes."

"Strange! Very strange!" said Min-ne-too-ka.

"Follow me," said the chief.

"No, I can't," said the maiden; "I am too weak, and must have food."

"Very true," replied the chief, "then remain here until we return."

In a moment they were gone. Min-ne-too-ka could not believe her senses; she must have been dreaming. Had she been talking with veritable men, or was her brain on fire? She emerged from her seclusion, looked out on nature—all was beautiful. Why this affliction? Just then the chief and War-ka-non made their appearance, and in their hands were fresh fish, duck, and a piece of deer. "Take, cook and eat," they exclaimed, and Min-ne-too-ka built a fire, dressed the game, cooked it, and in company with her companions, eat heartily of the food so providentially placed before her.

"Come," said the chief, "now follow us," and they wound down that path, said my informant, crossed that brook, passed over that trail, all in sight of where you sit, to the edge of the lake, where they found a canoe, into which they embarked, and then, without noise or paddles, the boat skimmed the water and touched the opposite shore. Entering the woods, they were in the city of the dead—Wa-kan. They traveled a short distance, when they came to an open space and then halted. Here lay the bones of their ancestors and their relatives, especially those who fell by the hands of the Chippewas. The tall and thick trees shut out the sunlight—all was calm, and silent and grand. The chief and his companions moved toward the open space and selecting a somewhat secluded spot, paused.

"Look, Min-ne-too-ka," he said, "but utter no word. Be not afraid." The coy maiden trembled with fear. She was in the hands of an invisible power; she tried to break away and run, but could not. She tried to scream, but could not, so, standing between the chief and War-ka-non, she patiently awaited what might follow. Presently a phosphorescent light gleamed among the trees; she saw her own people quietly reposing in and about their tepees; she saw her own self, when all of a sudden a wild war-whoop burst upon the air; she grasped at her companions, but they melted away under her hands. She could not endure the revolting sight! She tried to speak, but her lips were glued. Then came the infuriated savages; then followed the massacre; then she saw War-ka-non seize her around the waist, and then—all was dark. She turned and looked; her companions were gone and the scene faded from her view.

Min-ne-too-ka was almost wild with excitement. What did all this mean? Was it a reality or a dream? How should she get out of this dreadful entanglement? Turning, she moved a few steps to the right, when her mother stood before her, so real, so calm, so gentle, so loving, that she involuntarily stretched out her arms to greet her, but the voice came back: "Touch me not; I am your mother. I come to comfort you; I come to assure you that you are in the hands and under the control of Indian spirits. They will protect you. The scene you have just witnessed will be followed by another scene, and in it you can draw a moral lesson of the results of crime. Be not afraid, your father, mother, sisters and brothers are about you, and the chief and War-ka-non will protect you from all harm." With a smile of sweetness the figure gradually faded away, and Min-ne-too-ka looked out again on the cold, black trees, the little mounds that covered the bones of the dead, and the dismal, brooding darkness, that, like a black pall encircled her light and beautiful form.

"Min-ne-too-ka is afraid," said the chief, as he and War-ka-non appeared on either side of her. "No harm come to Min-ne-too-ka. Min-ne-too-ka is governed, guided, protected by spirit band. Min-ne-too-ka good. Look!"

The darkness was dissipated by another flash of phosphorescent light, when off in the distance could be seen a beautiful country, with trees, brooks, lakes, deer, birds, flowers, sunlight, and reposing in peaceful plenty, Min-ne-too-ka saw the twenty-nine victims of Chippewa brutality, and standing out in bold relief from all the rest, was one odd one, which she recognized as War-ka-non, the Chippewa brave, who had saved her from a cruel death. The scene was so peaceful, the faces so happy, as they gazed affectionately upon her, the country so lovely, that she lost all fear, and looking up into War-ka-non's face, beseeched him to let her go. Oh, how she longed to be at rest in that beautiful land.

"No, Min-ne-too-ka," said War-ka-non, smiling serenely down upon her, "not yet. Your mission is not yet filled. War-ka-non go with Min-ne-too-ka to the happy hunting ground when destiny ends her career here."

"See! Min-ne-too-ka," said the chief, pointing to the left—"see!" And off in the darkness Min-ne-too-ka observed a black, rolling river, and across it lay the trunk of a tree, and on this tree were several dark-visaged Indians, some trying to walk over to the other side, others were in the act of falling; several floundered in the water, which was full of toads, lizards and snakes; some driven back by the good spirits from the other shore, but all in turmoil, distress, darkness and woe! What a scene! It chilled the blood of the fair maiden, and she crept up closer to the side of War-ka-non and shuddered at the sight before her.

"That rolling water," said the chief, "is the river of death. In its turbulent waves can be found everything horrible to the feelings of the Indian. That tree is the bridge. When the good Indian dies, he passes over the bridge in safety into the happy hunting ground, but when the bad Indian dies, the spirits grease the tree, and he falls into the stream below. These Indians did a wanton, cruel wrong, and are reaping their reward."

Min-ne-too-ka's eyes sparkled with excitement; the warm blood gushed through the tawny skin of her cheek, and her little frame quivered, as she exclaimed: "I see clearly; I see it all; I will obey your bidding; I will consecrate myself to the wishes of my spirit friends, but oh, remove that horrible scene." The chief gave a wave of his hand and the picture disappeared, and all was again damp, and dark, and clammy, and desolate.

"Come," said the chief. "Come," said War-ka-non, looking down into the face of his now more than ever lovely Indian expectant bride, "come, go with us;" and they struck into a small trail that led out from the city of the dead to the banks of the lake and into the pure sunshine, where the birds were singing, the ducks were flying, the deer were bounding, the flowers were blooming, the trees nodding, and the gentle breeze, as it came from off the lake, cooled the feverish brow of the Indian girl as she followed her spirit guides. They passed westward to the extreme chain of lakes, ascended gradually a hill covered with tall, noble trees, wound down around the brow of a mound, at the base of which, nestling in a bower of beauty, and close to a rippling stream, were several Indian tepees.

"Go in among your Sioux friends and seek rest," said her companions, pointing to the scene below, and then they instantly disappeared.

Min-ne-too-ka approached the Indian settlement with

great timidity, was met cautiously, told her story, was cordially greeted and hospitably entertained; and here, amid all this regal beauty of nature's grandest handiwork, with the charm of a quiet retreat, with consciousness that she was beyond the reach of harm, the poor, weary, hungry, desolate orphan Indian girl found many hours of unalloyed pleasure, and peace, and happiness.

The old chief, who thus graphically gave me this narrative, stopped several times in the course of his story, poked the embers of the smoldering fire, refilled his pipe, gave several "ughs," and seemed deeply interested in the fate of the unfortunate Min-ne-too-ka.

"Over there," said the chief, pointing to the east side of the lake, "was the home of the Chippewas. Early in the day of one beautiful May morning, a Sioux maiden made her way toward their camp, well knowing that if once discovered her temerity would cost her her life. As she approached a tepee, inhabited only by three of her own sex, her courage failed; she paused, and turned to retrace her steps, when a Chippewa brave stood before her. It was the spirit form of War-ka-non.

"Why falters Min-ne-too-ka?" he asked. "No harm comes to Min-ne-too-ka. Her duty performed, she will join War-ka-non in the happy-hunting ground."

Min-ne-too-ka was surprised, awed into silence, and, feeling that she had not shown the faith she ought to have done in her noble and devoted lover—for she had now become dearly attached to him—exclaimed: "I will never falter again; thy will shall be done," and pressed forward to the camp of her inveterate enemy. Strange as it may appear, the Chippewa women received her, not, however, without great caution, and on the return of the warriors a council was held as to her fate. Why let a single member of their hated tribe live? The council decided she should die. Min-ne-too-ka begged one request—that she might appear among the Chippewa braves and demonstrate that she was innocent of all harm. The request was granted, and the next morning the young girl stood in the presence of her savage foes, and told them how she had been saved by War-ka-non—how she loved War-ka-non—how the great spirit had come to her—had shown her the happy hunting-ground—how the fate of the murderers had been pictured, and in most eloquent tones, begged of the warriors to drop the war-club, the scalping-knife, and the tomahawk, and deal justly and fairly with their enemy. She impressed upon them the sure fate of their bad acts—the reward of their good deeds, and so wrought upon their savage hearts that they began to relent, when, in a moment, War-ka-non stood by her side. When the Indians saw him they all fell to the ground, for they knew it was his spirit.

He said: "My people, you know War-ka-non! I come from the spirit land. I saw Min-ne-too-ka. I loved Min-ne-too-ka. She comes to you to impress you with the necessity of good deeds. The great Man-i-tou and War-ka-non are the friends of the lone Indian girl. Would you take her innocent life? Would you still make more crimson the river of blood that flows at your feet? My people, be good. My people, be just. My people, be kind. My people, hearken unto the voice of Min-ne-too-ka?"

In an instant he was gone, and left the Indian maiden standing alone in the council of her enemy, with their heads bowed to the earth and trembling with fear.

The morning dawned, and in the midst of the whole band of Chippewas—men, women, and children, who then occupied the eastern portion of the lake—stood Min-ne-too-ka. Hatred had turned to love—to adoration—to worship—and there, in the presence of that timid girl, and in the presence of the great spirit, the Indians resolved on a new and a better life; and from that day to this, said the old chief, the Chippewa nation have been firm friends of the whites, and brave, humane enemies of the Sioux.

"You see that tall, high knoll over there?" said the chief.

"What, the highest point on the lake?" I asked.

"Yes."

"Well, tradition has it that the next day after the marvelous meeting I have described, War-ka-non and Min-ne-too-ka were seen on the top of that knoll, and then, clasped together, they rose high in the air and floated over the lake in the plain view of hundreds of spectators, and finally entered the happy hunting-ground; and from that day to this it has been called Point Wa-kan, or the Supernatural, and is held in sacred memory by the Indians of both tribes."

It is thought, by many, that the lake derived its name from this beautiful Indian girl, who, though left an orphan and sorely tried by a series of misfortunes, was finally united to her devoted lover, and together they joined their many friends in that peaceful land beyond the river of death. And thus Min-ne-too-ka became Min-ne-ton-ka, or Beautiful Water.

THRILLING SCENES AND ADVENTURES AMONG THE INDIANS.

IT was a beautiful morning in June, 1863, when I asked the commander at our post for a detail of a company of men, with a captain, to acccompany me across the river to a place called Beaver Creek, where a whole white settlement had been cruelly massacred by the Indians the year before. This camp had been established for the collection of troops to compose an expedition against the Indians and drive them across the Missouri river. My object in making the trip was to gather information as to the amount of hay, corn and oats available for camp purposes, as I knew the Government would pay the heirs of the dead parties for losses incurred in the Indian raid, and that it was quite proper it should have the effects left behind by the unfortunate victims, to use for the troops then in the field. The morning was bright and glorious, and the company I had asked for was early on hand, the men happy in the thought of getting out of the dull routine of camp life, and eager to encounter any danger which might present itself. With an admonition from the commander of the garrison to keep together and watch every sign of danger (for the hostile Sioux were constantly hovering about us), the boys were ferried across the river to the east side, and wound up the hill to the plateau, which on the right stretched off into an unlimited prairie, and on the left was belted by woods, in which had been a settlement of some thirteen white families, now all dead!—the victims of savage brutality! It was my original purpose to go direct to Beaver Creek with the men, but learning that one of the soldiers had been in the campaign against the Indians the year previously, and that he knew the ground covered by the timber, I concluded to send Captain T. and his company across the prairie to the creek, and retain two men and reconnoitre for a short distance in the woods, promising that in an hour or so I would join the command where another settlement had existed, but which was now silent under the murderous attack of the savage foe. The soldiers were soon on their tramp across the plain, and with the two I had chosen to accompany me, we turned and entered the point of woods that skirted the river, and wound our way up to a small log house, dimly seen among the trees. Just before reaching it was a clearing, made by the former industrious, hardy pioneer, whose plow stood in the furrow, just where it was left when he was struck down by the infuriated Indians. Here was his broad-brimmed hat, cleft in two by the tomahawk; here was the whip where it fell; here was the poor, tattered coat, riddled with bullet holes. We approached the house. The doors were shattered; the windows were broken. We entered; what a scene! Here the poor victims had fought desperately for their lives. Broken chairs, broken tables, fragments of dresses, and blood-stained floors, clearly indicated how dreadful had been the fight of the pioneer to save his wife and little ones from the clutches of the savage demons who panted for their blood. Here, too, we found feathers from the beds that had been ripped open in search of treasure. The hay and oats stood in the stacks unmolested; the houses were grim and silent! All was still, except the moaning of the wind as it swept through the tree-tops, and sung a mournful dirge over the lamented dead.

Interested in these horrible scenes, we pushed on to the next house, where we found a similar state of affairs, only with this exception that, in lifting up a scuttle-door leading into the cellar, we beheld a ghastly skeleton of a little child, the living body of which had no doubt been put there by its fond parent for safe-keeping, but whose little form had wasted away by starvation. Its mother never returned. Again, we pushed on to the third house, forgetting the promise to Captain T. to be with him in an hour or so, but deeply interested in all we saw, when, recalling the fact that we must join our main body of men before dark, we retraced our steps and struck out on to the prairie in a direction, we thought, which led to Beaver Creek. On we traveled, with nothing to guide us, not even a twig as big as the finger of a man's hand, until we had made some three miles, when, conscious that we were lost, that it was useless to proceed any further, we came back into the woods, mortified at the blunder we had made. It was now about two o'clock in the afternoon, and it would be impossible to reach the creek in time to intercept Captain T., so I decided, as we did not know where we were, to make the most of it, go back to our original starting point, and proceed with my investigations in the belt of woods that skirted the river. House after house was passed and inspected, when we came to a ravine leading down to the river's edge. Here was pointed out to me, by one of the men, the spot where thirteen inhabitants had been overtaken in their flight the year before, murdered, and piled in one heap. A little distance from this point we came across the remains of a woman whose body had no doubt been overlooked by the expedition the previous year, and, after viewing it, we passed on and came to the last house in the belt. In this house were wooden shoes, crude wooden chairs, wooden cradles, clearly showing that the inmates were foreigners; but all was still—all had gone! the savage had done his work most completely—no sound broke the stillness of that twilight evening!

"Well, boys," I said, as we emerged from the woods and gazed out on to the wide prairie, broken only by a little rise of hills in the distance, "we are lost! We are in the neighborhood of where the Indians have been seen by our scouts very recently, and we have got to play our parts pretty nicely to get out of this bad scrape. How are your guns? All right? I have no weapon with me, not even a pistol!" "Never mind, Captain," said one of the boys, "you shall die behind our bodies." Of course I had to appear bold, although I trembled for my scalp, for I was conscious that we were in imminent danger, and how to get out of it was my great study. Beside, I had no business to leave the main command. If these two brave fellows, who were so willing to die for me, should fall by the Indians, I alone would be responsible for their deaths; and then I began to realize how foolish I would be considered at camp, and so, wrought up to a very high pitch of excitement, I was determined to baffle the Indians and save the lives of my men as well as my own.

The sun was just sinking behind the hills, and threw

a glinter across the prairie, when I said to John, "Go out carefully on to the plain; look in every direction and mark what you see, for we must make our way out from here immediately, and creep along to where we first entered the timber. Say nothing, but report privately to me." While he was gone, I ascended a gradual rise of ground, and with my eye swept the horizon. Just off to the right I thought I saw an Indian head bob up and down, but dismissed the matter from my mind as a part of a distorted imagination. John soon returned, and, in a cool, yet decided tone, informed me that he saw a human being's head peep up just over the little rise at the left. "All right, my boy," I remarked; "take up a position over there and listen; tell me if you hear anything." Calling Bill, who was as true and trusty as steel, I said: "Go out cautiously about a quarter of a mile; watch every point of the compass, return, and tell me what you see." In the meantime I chose what I considered the best place to get out on the prairie, for if we were watched we would be obliged to leave the timber at once. Returning, Bill gave the same information as John; so, cautioning the boys to keep quiet, mark every noise, and let nothing escape their attention, I ventured out myself, and true enough, just over the brow of a little hill, an Indian could be plainly seen to rise, then dodge, then run and dodge again. We were watched by the enemy.

"Boys, examine your guns! See if they are all right. Look to your ammunition. Keep cool. Darkness is coming, and with it the red devils. We must crawl out from here under the cover of night, and then make our way, as best we can, toward the river, for I am satisfied the Indians are on our track." Each one separated from the other, and worked his way on to the prairie, fortunately to a ravine, made by the water in the spring. In this ravine and under its banks several places had been worn out by the rain, and into these places, separately, we all crept, pulling the tall, dead grass over us, thus shielding ourselves from observation. Soon we could hear the dull, heavy tread of the Indians—some ten in number—and then the sound came nearer and nearer; then it echoed in the woods; then it came again out on to the prairie; then it drew still nearer; then we could hear the enemy talking; and I overheard, in Indian, the remark, "they must be here." Then the heavy tread of a warrior came within two feet of where I lay. He stopped; he listened. I did not breathe. Cold perspiration came out all over me. He poked his gun within a foot of my body. He peeked into the hiding places of my comrades, and then, as if satisfied, gave a grunt and sullenly joined his companions, who were only ten feet off, in consultation as to what they should do. We had foiled the Indians, inasmuch as we had crawled upon our stomachs and left no footprints behind, and yet any minute might reveal our hiding places. Such agony of suspense! Such a moment of life! We heard the well-known savage word, "marshon," and then one after another they fell into line, and their steady tread grew fainter and fainter, until entirely lost to the ear. Not a word had been spokon; not a quiver made; still as death we lay in our places, as if on the verge of the grave. We did not dare to move or speak, for we knew Indian character well enough to be assured that one of their number might be just over us, and instant death follow. Thirty minutes had elapsed, but not a word had been uttered, when I essayed, in a faint voice, to call, "Bill?" "All right," said Bill. "John?" "Steady," was the reply. We crept out slyly; gazed into the darkness; put our ears to the ground; moved cautiously forward, paused, listened, and then satisfied that our path was clear, made our way back to the old house in the woods, secreted ourselves until morning, and then a new surprise met us in the neigh of Indian ponies. Bill discovered, however, that these ponies were neither saddled nor bridled, and all at once it dawned upon our brains that we must be in the vicinity of our friendly Indian scouting camp. Leaving our hiding-places, we ascended a small mound about half a mile in the distance, and there just beyond we saw the stockade of our scouts, and in a blessed few minutes after we were inside the inclosure, the guests of our trusty dusky friends, who laughed heartily over the story we told of our hair-breadth escape from the savage foe. Night passed, and at early morning, knowing full well that the camp would be in great commotion if we did not make our appearance, we mounted Indian ponies, and accompanied by two friendly Indian guides, started off in a brisk gallop for the river, hailed the ferryman, was conveyed across, and entered the camp just as the troops were leaving in every direction to search for our dead bodies. Mounted men were immediately sent out to recall the soldiers, hundreds of "boys in blue" gathered about us to hear our story, and to all appearances there was great rejoicing over the fact that the Commissary and Quartermaster of the post and his two faithful men had returned to the camp safe and sound.

The next day Bill came to me and asked for a piece of planed board, about four feet high by one and a half wide. "No," I said, "Bill, I can't let you have it. There are nearly four thousand soldiers in camp, and as every man wants a piece of board, by granting their requests I won't have lumber enough to build with." As he turned to go away, I noticed a peculiar sadness on his countenance, and I called him back. "What do you want this board for?" He replied, "You remember the dead body of that woman we saw yesterday?" "Yes." "You remember I examined the ring on her finger, her teeth, her dress?" "Yes." "Well, that was my mother!" "Your mother! how in heaven is that?" "Well, my parents lived here before I entered the army. Last year we found all my family dead but my mother. She must have made an effort to fly, was shot where she fell, and her body has remained until yesterday undiscovered. I want the board to place at the head of her grave when I bury her!" The appeal was so touching, that I ordered my carpenter to make the board; Bill lettered it, and the next day, in company with ten well-armed men, he repaired to the spot where his mother met her death, buried the body, and returned to his duty with a solemn resolution to avenge the murder of his whole family, even if it should take a lifetime. He faithfully kept his resolution, for, years afterward, when I met him, just returned from the frontier, he assured me he had killed twenty Indians and was good for twenty more. Who could blame him?

A recent writer, speaking of this same man, says: "Commanche Bill, or William Porter, is forty-seven years of age, but looks much younger. He wears the proverbial long hair, cropped closer behind than many who affect this style. He is not over five feet ten inches in height, with a broad chest and brawny arms, and an iron frame, which fatigue cannot overcome nor exertion subdue. He is taciturn almost to a fault, and loth to speak of himself. In the far West his reputation as a guide, scout and interpreter, is great, and he looks with scorn on lesser luminaries and other would-be heroes."

William Porter was born of Scotch parents, in Iowa, removed to Minnesota, above New Ulm, and lived there until the troublesome times of 1862, when his whole family was massacred.

"Haven't you a sister yet living in Minnesota?"

"Thar ain't a drop of my blood flowin' in the veins of any living human bein'," was the sad response. He then told the story of the massacre of his mother and sister, and the eyes of the sturdy plainsman were suffused with something which looked like tears.

"I tell you it's enough to make a man a demon," he said; "father, mother, sister, two cousins, an uncle, aunt and wife killed at one blow. I remember that little mother; she wan't bigger'n your fist, and she loved me as a Scotch mother can love. She used to say to father: 'William's getting too big for you to handle,' but she could do anything with me. I remember she came to me and said: 'Well, there's a kiss from your mither, lad,' and when I came back she lay killed by them red devils. I tell you, boys, it made a demon out of me," and the strong man pressed his hands to his head, and threw back his long hair with a wild gesture in the agony of the awful revelation.

"Who killed your mother, Bill?"

"It was one of Cut Nose's band."

"Is he alive yet?"

"Well, I guess he will never scalp any more women."

"Did they kill your wife, too?"

"Yes; they tortured her to death! Oh! I've had a scalp for every drop of blood they spilled that day. I took an oath that as long as I could look through the hind sight of a rifle, I'd kill every Sioux I got a chance to shoot at, and you bet I have kept my oath."

And this was Bill, one of the men who was with the writer and crawled out on to the prairie, and saw that Indian head bobbing up and down, and who subsequently arrived, with the author, safe in camp. He has kept his oath, for he has killed not less than twenty-five Indians, and, under all the circumstances, who can blame him?

MAIDEN ROCK;

OR, "THE LOVER'S LEAP."

"SINCE my remembrance," said an old Chief to Major Long, in the year 1860, a large part of the Sioux Indians of La Feuelle's band, had been in the habit of making annual visits from the river St. Peter to Prairie du Chien. When the party in question arrived at the hill, now called the Lover's Leap, or, more properly, Maiden Rock, they stopped to gather blue clay, which is found near the foot of the hill, for the purpose of painting themselves. Of this party was the young Indian maiden who is the subject of this legend.

She had for a long time received the addressed of a young hunter, who had formed an unconquerable attachment for her, and for whom she entertained the strongest affection. Her parents and brothers were strenuously opposed to her choice and warmly seconded the solicitations of a young warrior, who was very much beloved by the Indian nation, for his bravery and other good qualities. To obviate her objection to the warrior as being destitute of the means of clothing and feeding her in consequence of the life he must lead in order to perform the duties of his profession, her brothers agreed to be at the expense of providing everything that was necessary for the ease and comfort of a family, and presented them to the young warrior. This they did on the day of their arrival at the fatal spot, with the hope that their sister would readily be prevailed upon to marry the young man whom all her objections to were thus obviated. She still persisted, however, in the determination never to marry any but the object of her sincere affection, while her parents and brothers finding they could not accomplish their purpose by gentle means, began to treat her with severity. They insisted upon her compliance with their wishes, still summoning the argument of filial duty and affection in aid of their cause. She replied: "I do not love the soldier and would live single forever rather than marry him. You call me daughter and sister, as if this should induce me to marry the man of your choice and not my own. You say you love me, yet you have driven the only man that can make me happy, far from me. He loved me, but you would not let us be happy together. He has therefore left me; he has left his parents and all his friends and gone to bewail in the woods. He cannot partake of the pleasure of this party. He can do nothing but mourn. You are not satisfied with all this. You have not made me miserable enough. You would now compel me to marry a man I do not love. Since this is your purpose, let it be so. You will soon have no daughter or sister to torment or beguile with your false professions of love."

The same day was fixed upon as the day of her marriage with the warrior, and the Indians were busily occupied in getting clay and painting themselves preparatory for the nuptial ceremony. She, in the meantime, walked aside from the rest of the party, ascended to the top of the hill known as Maiden Rock, located on the Upper Mississippi, called aloud to her parents and brothers, upbraiding them for their unkind treatment: "You refused to let me marry agreeably to my own choice. You then endeavored by artifice to unite me to a man I cannot love, and now you will force me to marry him whether I will or not. You thought to allure and make me wretched, but you shall be disappointed." Her parents, aware of her design to throw herself over the precipice, ran to the foot of the hill and entreated her to desist, with all the tenderness and concern that parental fondness could suggest, tearing their hair and bewailing in the bitterest manner, while her brothers attempted to gain the summit before she should execute her fatal purpose. But all in vain. She was determined and resolute. She commenced singing her death song, and immediately threw herself headlong down the precipice, preferring certain and instantaneous death to a lingering state of unhappy wedlock. And thus comes the tradition of "Maiden Rock, or Lover's Leap."

I learn from other sources, outside of the Chief's narrative, as given by Major Long, that when the hunter-lover, Kad-da-lus-ka, heard of the tragic death of We-no-na, he reciprocated her devotion by jumping into the river, and according to Indian belief, passed safely over the barrier of death, and the two lovers were seen afterward by their friends, traveling hand in hand in the happy hunting ground.

It is alleged by parties who have remained at the foot of Maiden Rock all night, that about twelve o'clock a low, plaintive wail is heard, at first almost inaudible, but soon after gathering in volume, the sound breaks out into a wild, unearthly song, which floats out on to the water and reverberates among the hills, and then a slight, beautiful female figure appears on the top of the rock, and swaying to and fro, for a few moments, keeping time with her voice, it plunges suddenly headforemost, and then a sickening thug sound is heard, and all is still! One of the earliest and perhaps one of the best authenticated Indian legends, is that of MAIDEN ROCK.

LAKE PEPIN AND ITS SCENERY.

LAKE PEPIN is a body of water in the Mississippi river—in fact the lake is merely a distension of the river—some five miles wide and some twenty-five miles long. Wabashaw is at the lower end of the lake, and is noted in Indian history as a favorite place of the Sioux, where, under the leadership of their chief after whom the city is named, they held their councils, delared their wars, smoked their pipes, uttered their outbursts of eloquence, danced their dances, and otherwise made it the elegant capital of their people. Frontenac is at the head of the lake, and looking out from this charming spot, the eye of the traveler rests upon some of the grandest scenery in the world. We not only find many traces of the existence of Indians above Lake Pepin, but we find many relics of a people far older than even the red men themselves—the mound builders of a pre-historic age. Indeed, I am told, that in a mound I visited some three hundred feet above the Mississippi river, below Winona, the bones of a gigantic warrior were found, reaching eight feet in height, and in his skull was a copper tomahawk with a tempered edge, showing that the people of that day possessed an art now lost to the present age, viz: that of hardening copper, so as to make it available for cutting purposes, the same as steel. Evidences of these mounds, especially near Wabashaw and even below it, are abundant. So, too, there are evidences of a people who at one time were engaged in smelting lead ore, traces of which are quite apparent.

The high uplifts of rocks, their grotesque character, the dark ravines, the diversified scenery, which marks the borders of the river, with the grand river itself, make a ride on the broad bosom of the Father of Waters not only delightful, but deeply interesting to the lover of romance as well as to the lover of research. The bluffs on the West side of the river rise to a height of from 475 to 500 feet. About midway of Lake Pepin (which, as I have already said, is a part of the Mississippi river itself), can be seen a prominent peak, well known to tourists as MAIDEN ROCK, and here is the point from whence an Indian maiden precipitated herself 400 feet to the base below, rather than marry a man she did not love. Most Indian legends partake of the fabulous, with only a little tincture of truth to make them palatable, but it *is* a fact that an Indian girl DID throw herself from this rock, and for the reason already given, but it is NOT a fact that it was an Indian she loved, but a Frenchman. John Bush, eighty-three years of age, writes as follows:

"Now, as for Maiden Rock being a legend, it is a mistake. It was a real thing and no legend. The man who wanted to marry the girl was a young Frenchman. He was killed by lightning. I saw him ten minutes after he was killed. He was a young man then. The men who knew about it are all dead but myself."

So this legend, or romance passes out of fiction into reality, and of course becomes more interesting as it becomes known to be a fact, supported by the evidence of a living witness.

Maiden Rock itself is a peculiar freak of nature. It appears to have been shot up from below and then squared by the compass. The surroundings are wild and weird, with a few straggling, stunted trees, and it seems to be a fitting place for the spirit of the Indian girl to roam with her lover—as it is alleged she does—outside and beyond the tantalizing influences of her relatives, who, in their day sought to do what the whites now seek to do, to make proper matches for the young people, in order to increase the standing, the influence, and in many cases the wealth of their children.

The tourist, as he ascends the river on the deck of the steamer, can see Maiden Rock looming up into the clouds. He catches the rugged scenery, the peerless buttes, the smooth, grand expanse of the lake; then the flowing river, the numerous boats and rafts that dot its bosom, and if he is a lover of nature in her grandest type, he will become etherealized, as it were, and electrified by the surpassing beauty of the American scenery, as seen in a trip up the Mississippi river to the capital city of a great empire which lies beyond.

KIS-SE-ME-PA AND KAR-GO-KA.

EVERY spring, for perhaps a century, or as long as there has been a nation of red men, an island in the middle of White Bear lake had been visited by a band of Indians for the purpose of making maple sugar.

Tradition says that many years ago, while the Indians were upon this island, a young warrior loved and wooed the daughter of his chief, and it is said, also, the maiden loved the warrior. He had again and again been refused her hand by her parents, the old chief alleging that he was no brave, and his old consort calling him a woman!

The sun had again set upon the "sugar bush," and the bright moon rode high in the blue heavens, when the young warrior took down his flute and went out alone, once more to sing the story of his love. The mild breeze gently moved the two gay feathers in his head dress, and as he mounted upon the trunk of a leaning tree, the damp snow fell from his feet heavily. As he raised his flute to his lips his blanket slipped from his well-formed shoulders, and lay partly on the snow beneath. He began his wild, weird love song, but soon felt that he was cold, and as he reached back for his blanket some unseen hand laid it gently on his shoulders. It was the hand of his love—his guardian angel. She took her place beside him, and for the present they were happy;—for the Indian has a heart to love, and in this respect he is as noble as in his own freedom, which makes him the child of the forest. As the legend runs, a large white bear, thinking, perhaps, that polar snows and dismal winter extended everywhere, took up his journey southward. He at length reached the northern shore of the lake which now bears his name, walked down the bank, and made his way noiselessly through the deep, heavy snow toward the island. The lovers had left their first retreat, and were seated among the branches of a large elm which hung far out over the lake. For fear of being detected they had talked almost in a whisper, and now, that they might get back to camp in good time and thereby avoid suspicion, they were just rising to return, when the maiden uttered a shriek which was heard at the camp, and bounding toward the young brave, she caught his blanket, but missed the direction of her foot and fell, bearing the blanket with her into the great arms of the ferocious monster, which had crawled stealthily under the tree. Instantly every man, woman and child of the band were upon the island, but all unarmed. Cries and wailings went up from every mouth. What was to be done? In the meantime this white and savage beast held the breathless maiden in his huge grasp, and fondled with his precious prey as if he were used to scenes like this. One deafening yell from the lover warrior is heard above the cry of hundreds of his tribe, and dashing away to his wigwam, only a few steps distant, he grasps his faithful knife, returns almost at a single bound to the scene of fear and fright, rushes out along the leaning tree to the spot where his treasure fell, and springing with the fury of a mad panther, pounced upon his prey. The animal turned, and with one stroke of his huge paw brought the lovers heart to heart, but the next moment the warrior, with one plunge of the blade of his knife, opened the crimson sluices of death, and the dying bear relaxed his hold.

That night there was no more sleep for the band or the lovers, and as the young and the old danced about the carcass of the dead monster and feasted upon his flesh, the gallant warrior was presented with another plume, and ere another moon had set he had a living treasure added to his heart. Their children for many years played upon the tanned skin of the WHITE BEAR —from which the lake derives its name—and the maiden and the brave remembered long the fearful scene and the rescue that made them one, for Kis-se-me-pa and Kar-go-ka could never forget their fearful encounter with the huge monster that came so near sending them to the happy hunting ground.

NARROW ESCAPE FROM A HORRIBLE INDIAN MASSACRE.

THE SKULKING DOG.

IN the spring of 1863 I was stationed at Camp Pope, above Fort Ridgely, on the Minnesota river, State of Minnesota, in the double capacity of United States Commissary and Quartermaster. This was after the terrible Indian massacre, whereby nearly one thousand innocent settlers lost their lives by the savages, and after the Government had organized a command of soldiers, under a competent leader, to pursue the hostile Sioux, reclaim the white prisoners, but at any rate drive the enemy into or across the Missouri river, where arrangements had been made to intercept, and if possible, annihilate them.

Camp Pope was situated above Little Crow's village, where the chief of that name had resided, and was in the neighborhood of where the Indian war had been inaugurated, for it was Little Crow himself who marshaled his young warriors to battle, and who was responsible for the horrid butcheries of the whites the previous year. The camp was located some distance from the Minnesota river, overlooked by a ridge of bluffs, with drift granite boulders on the right, and a very pretty valley stretching off up toward Yellow Medicine, the former Indian agency. The place was devoid of trees and seemed admirably adapted to the purpose for which it was chosen, with one exception.

On the right of the camp, looking down toward the Minnesota river, was a thick clump of bushes, and I remember expressing fears when the camp was selected, that the Indians might, under cover of these bushes, especially after the leaves came out, make an attack upon it, but men of greater Indian experience than myself, thought, that by throwing out a guard in that direction, that all surprise could be anticipated, so the camp soon became a young city of bustling life and activity. At last, in June, 1863, the entire command, comprising 4,000 soldiers, with all the necessary essentials for a successful campaign against the hostile savages, set out on its journey, and winding up in the valley already indicated, and passing over the bluff, made an imposing and stirring scene.

Never did I experience a more lonely or a more homesick feeling, as when, towards sundown of that memorable day, I looked out upon that deserted camp, where, only ten hours before, four thousand soldiers, with eighteen hundred horses and mules; with the tread of men, with martial music, with familiar faces, with burning camp fires, with white tents, and streaming flags, were wont to greet my eye—all now gone!—desolate, dark, lonely, dreary! How still! How I longed for wings to fly to get away from myself!—what a terrible depression came upon me! and with a shudder I turned and sought my office, where consolation was to come only in sleep.

Camp Pope was the rendezvous for supplies which might be needed for the expedition after it had left, and for the sick which might be sent back from it. Also for disabled horses and other property belonging to the Government. A small stockade of logs had been thrown up in case of an attack from the Indians, and inside of this defense was Company I, of the Ninth Regiment, a class of boys who had never smelt Indian gun-powder, and from what I could learn, who really never wanted to, and yet they were all brave men. In the Quartermaster's building was a small squad of soldiers, called the convalescent corps, unfit for duty, but who, in case of an emergency, might be made available. Of eleven horses, not more than two could be put to any use, whatever, and these were kept in readiness in case of an attack. An occasional Indian (no doubt a spy) would peer in upon the camp, but notwithstanding the vigilance of the soldiers, he would contrive to escape.

About ten days after the expedition had left rumors came from the Indian scout-camp, some miles above our own, that tracks of Indian ponies had been seen on the west side of the Minnesota river, and fears were entertained that an attack might be made upon us at any moment. These rumors gained credence, because we all thought it would be a very Indian-like trick to slip round behind the expedition, and pounce in upon our small party; and if any considerable number of Indians had done so, the writer, and many others, would have been *non est*, while the savages would have gained one scalp minus the hair; and therein I always considered I should get the better of our wily enemy, who, I imagined, would grit his teeth as he held up his trophy of a bald and shining pate, out of which he could get no further satisfaction than a—grunt. (Indians don't like bald-headed men.)

The constant fear of an attack had induced the commander of the post to take every precautionary measure for defense he could. I had brought the horses inside the guard-lines; trenches had been dug about the Commissary and Quartermaster's buildings, while a camp-fire was kept constantly burning inside of the stockade, where our most available men were quartered. The command was so small that only four guards and reliefs could be employed to protect the camp, and, as every day brought confirmatory news of Indians hovering about us, these guards were instructed to watch carefully, and, on the first appearance of any object, halt it three times, and, on the last time, if it did not halt, fire. All parties, being satisfied that an unexpected attack could not be made upon the camp, settled down to quietness and to rest.

It was evening. The sky was overcast with black clouds, and the darkness was almost impenetrable. The wind soughed around the camp, and moaned like some lost spirit, anxious to gain admittance into my little office, where I sat revelling upon the past. Ever and anon, amid the death-like stillness of the night, only the click of a musket could be heard to break the eternal monotony of the blast, as it came in fitful gusts and painted, in imagination, the unrelenting, wandering, dancing skeletons of the red men, who had arisen from their graves to take part in the coming conflict! To me they seemed dodging around the corners, and peeping into the windows, and gathering at the camp-fire, and yet, calm and serene, amid all this outside clamor, I dreamed of home, and friends and loved ones. In an instant my reveries were disturbed by the report of a gun, and seizing my pistol, I emerged into the darkness. In a minute more the camp was all astir, for all realized the impending and probable danger, and pushing my way rapidly to the camp-fire in the stockade, I met the officer in command, with his hair in many kinks, shirt bosom open, coat off, with no shoes or stockings (it was a warm night in June), and who hurriedly exclaimed:

"Captain, where do you think that report came from?"

I replied, "Guard No. 4. Think they are after our horses."

"No; I think it came from No. 3," he answered, and off he darted into the darkness, leaving me making my way, as fast as possible, to the stockade. In the meantime the soldiers gathered around the camp-fire, and as the light shone upon their pale and frightened faces, the scene was one of a most impressive character. Here I halted, but no news coming from the commander of the post, and fearing that not only he but all the guards had been shot down by arrows, and that any minute we might see the infuriated redskins rushing in upon us, with their war-whoops, tomahawks and knives, I ordered two soldiers to accompany me, and crawling upon our hands and knees, some distance from each other (so that we might not be shot at once), we felt our way in the darkness, to guard No. 4, where we heard subdued voices, and on drawing nearer, found them to be that of the guard and the faithful commander, wo had periled his own life to save that of his command. An explanation followed, to the effect that the guard, who was a half-breed Indian, had discovered a large dog crawling up from the bushes previously alluded to, and that, after halting him three times, he fired, and the animal ran back to the spot from whence he came. We all returned to camp, or rather the stockade, but there was no sleep that night. Every man was on the alert for the enemy.

A few days after this event news came that Little Crow, who had instigated the war, had been shot near Glencoe, and that his son, who, in the meantime had been captured, stated that his father and seventeen other Indians had decided to take our camp at the time the animal was seen to ascend the hill, and for that purpose had sent forward an Indian in a dog's skin, who was to crawl up to and shoot down the guard with arrows, and then the other Indians were to surprise the command and murder every soul! Had it not been for the sagacity and faithfulness of this half-breed guard, the devilish purpose of Little Crow might have been accomplished, but, finding the camp alarmed through the report of the gun, he and his men made their way toward the settlements near Glencoe to steal horses, where he finally met his death. And thus we escaped a horrible butchery from the same savages, who, but a short time before, had murdered one thousand inoffensive white citizens, escaped simply through the sagacity of a half-breed guard, who, knowing Indian character better than the whites, fired at the dodging animal, which, in the skin of a dog, proved to be a tried warrior of the great Sioux chieftain, who was only waiting with his men to hear that our sentinels had been killed by the silent arrows from his disguised savage soldier, to complete the slaughter of the whole camp! But, in the language of Webster—"We still live."

PICK-A-WA-KA AND EL-MO-NA.

MANY moons ago large tribes of Indians used to roam over the ground now known as Elmo Park. The tribes were hostile to each other, and never let an opportunity pass to visit vengeance upon their enemy. Both were wily and warlike, the Sioux noted for their cunning and bravery, the Chippewas for their superior manly qualities, but both were ever on the alert to visit death upon their deadly foe. Near where a hotel now stands, and amid a bower of trees and brush, was located a modest, silent tepee, and in it on a bright moonlight night, singing a low, plaintive love song, was a beautiful Sioux maiden. Her subdued, sweet, wild tones floated over the water, and ever and anon she peered out into space as though expecting some visitor, and yet, as she thought of his comiug her frame quivered and she shrank back into her quiet home as though some dreadful danger was impending. Again she sang. Again her eye brightened. She placed her ear to the pebbly shore and listened, and then like a beautiful fawn she seemed transfixed to the spot. Hark! How still! Listen! She hears again! How her heart beats! Away off on the other side of the lake can be heard the light dipping of paddles! How faint and yet how clear to her, his signal!

A mile back of her tepee is her band. The warriors are dancing over the scalps of the Chippewas. They are drunk with excitement. They hear nothing, know nothing, but blood; and so, seeking her opportunity she has gained her silent retreat; she has made her presence known to her lover, and he is coming—not one of her own band—not one of her own tribe, but a gallant hero of her deadly enemies—no less than a young warrior of the Chippewa nation; for love laughs at all restraints, even among the rude children of the forests. Nearer and nearer the light canoe glides silently to the shore. It stops, and with a bound a noble youth springs to the side of the maiden. He clasps her in his arms. Looking down into her dark eyes, he says:

"El-mo-na! we have met again, and ere another moon passes we shall be one. Oh! my necarnis—(best friend)—how beautiful to know that amid all the strife of our tribes, two hearts know naught but love!"

"Pick-a-wa-ka, be brave!" said El-mo-na. "He comes among danger! Hear my people? Pick-a-wa-ka's heart, be big! See the moonlight kissing the ripples? El-mo-na's heart kisses Pick-a-wa-ka!" And there, standing upon the shore of this lake, in a spot so quiet, so beautiful, so secluded, yet so dangerous, with the waves singing a gentle lullaby, the moonbeams playing with the foliage of the trees, the Indian lovers pledged their hearts, and calling upon the Great Spirit to witness their fidelity, clasped each other in an embrace of eternal love.

List! a sound is heard in the distance! El-mo-na trembles! She beseeches Pick-a-wa-ka to fly for his life! They are discovered! The young Chippewa brave draws his left arm about his love, shielding her with his person, and with his right hand grasps his knife. With a wild war-whoop the Sioux are upon him! Their tomahawks gleam in the moonbeams! They draw nearer and nearer! The fatal stroke descends, when, with the agility of a tigress, El-mo-na glides in front of him and the knife enters her body, and she falls to the ground. Relieved of his burden, Pick-a-wa-ka is soon conscious of his power. Desperate with the belief that his love is mortally wounded, he dashes at his enemies, and almost instantly the two assailants lie dead upon the beach. But more of the band is coming! He has no time to lose. Picking up the lifeless body of El-mo-na, he placed it tenderly in the canoe, and in a moment more was paddling over the lake, and when his enemies had reached the shore, his boat was some distance from land. He rowed with superhuman power; reached the landing on the opposite side of the lake, near where a little stream ripples in laughter down the bank, bore his sacred trust to the camp of his tribe, and exhausted, fell senseless by its side. On recovering, a medicine man was bending over him, and near him sat El-mo-na, her dark, brilliant eyes fixed upon his face. Her wound did not prove fatal. With gentle nursing she fully recovered, married Pick-a-wa-ka, and years afterwards, when both her own tribe and the Chippewas were removed far away, and when eighty moons had silvered their hair with gray, they visited the haunts of their early love, secured permission to dwell in peace in a quiet, lovely spot not far from the present hotel, where they died, greatly esteemed by what few whites roamed through the country at that time in quest of game and fur.

It is said that on still moonlight nights a wild, sweet Indian song can be heard floating over the waters of the lake, supposed to be the spirit of El-mo-na, while a light canoe can be seen gliding noiselessly upon the waves as they gently dash against the shore. In honor of this beautiful Indian legend, no wonder the place is called—ELMO LODGE!

MEMORY OF A NOTED CHIPPEWA CHIEF—HOLE-IN-THE-DAY.

WHILE sitting in a small office of a hotel in the West, in the year 1853, or thirty-one years ago, my attention was attracted by the imposing presence of a large Indian chief, who, with his blanket about him, strode into the room with the dignity of a Roman Senator. He was a large man, with high cheek bones, a well-poised head, dark, brilliant black eyes and hair. With a pleasant smile, he exclaimed, as he passed—"Booshu, neches," or in Indian dialect—"how to do, friend?" and took a seat near me. There was a massive characteristic about the man which did not belong to the ordinary Indian, and yet he had all the Indian peculiarities. Dinner was soon announced and he took a seat near me at the table. He ate with ordinary deliberation, and an ordinary amount of food, but while thus engaged, one of the windows was suddenly darkened, and on looking up I beheld many grimmy faces and burning eyes, with war-paint and feathers, the possessors of which belonged to the Sioux nation—the deadly enemies of the noted chief. Gleaming knives and partially concealed tomahawks, made my position by the side of the warrior rather uncomfortable, so I moved away, but he continued to eat on, and then the door opened and thirty Sioux Indians filed along in front of the foe of their nation, with clinched rifles and hearts glowing with revenge. Still, calm, with not a muscle of his mobile face denoting fear, the chief finished his dinner, cooly arose, drew his blanket about him and with a lordly tread and a compressed lip, and flashing eyes, walked down in front of these hostile Sioux, and lighting his pipe, deliberately puffed the smoke into the very faces of his inveterate foe!

That man was Hole-in-the-Day, the great and noted chief of the Chippewa Nation, and the thirty Sioux warriors were on his war-path, but they well knew, and so did Hole-in-the-Day, that the moment a blow had been struck, that the white man's troops would dash down upon them and terminate their career; so the chief passed along in safety, and the sullen Sioux soon after withdrew to their own possessions, which, at that time, was on the west side of the Mississippi river. The wily chief well knew that his safety lay in the fact that he was on land belonging to the whites, while had he been on the other side of the river, on ground owned by the Sioux, he would have met a terrible death, as it was only a short time before he crossed the river, took two Sioux scalps, right in the face of the enemy and civilization, and returned glorying over his achievement. He was a brave, intelligent Indian chief, and his memory is kindly cherished by the whites.

GRAVE OF HOLE-IN-THE-DAY.

About two miles northwest of Little Falls, a town located on the Upper Mississippi river, in Minnesota, and on a high hill, known as Hole-in-the-Day's bluff, lies the body of the great Chippewa chief, and that of his father, a noted chief before him, both facing southeast, so they can watch the movements of their enemies —the Sioux. There is a gap between the depression of the two hills upon which the bodies lie, and in the middle of this depression stands a lone tree, conveying the idea from the road-side, that a sentinel was guarding the graves. The view from the top of this bluff is grand, presenting a scene unrivaled in beauty and charming naturalness. No other Indians are permitted to be buried near the remains of these two great Chippewa chieftains.

HE-LE-O-PA AND NIM-PE-WA-PA.

THERE is something peculiarly fascinating about an Indian tradition, handed down, as it it, not in books, but from father to son, while smoking their pipes around the wigwam fire; and there is something additionally charming in the story as told by the Indian himself. Some fifteen years ago, while on my way to the Canadian shore with a company of explorers, we camped on the banks of a beautiful sheet of water known as Me-de-wa-ka, when our "Ne-car-nis," or, in the Chippewa language, "our best friend"—that is, an Indian in the party who had attached himself to our person—entertained us, through my interpreter, with the following interesting legend:

"Many moons ago," said the Indian, with a whiff of his pipe, "a party of Sioux crept down silently to the shores of Me-de-wa-ka, and, gazing a moment, disappeared in the thick underbrush that encircled the lake."

And right here the reader should bear in mind that the Sioux and Chippewas have been at war for a century past, and that all the country on the east side of the Mississippi belonged to the Chippewas, while all the country on the west side belonged to the Sioux.

"A young Chippewa girl," continued the Indian, "beautiful as the fawn, with features radiant with perfection, was sitting upon the bank of the lake, toying with the gentle waves, as they came and kissed her tawny feet, but when she saw these enemies of her race, she screamed and ran to the tepee, which was located a little back from the shore, in a clump of trees.

Nim-pe-wa-pa, her lover, brave, gallant, affectionate, like a deer dashed from the wigwam, and, catching the maiden in his arms, asked, 'What fear?' He-le-o-pa pointed to the brush and tremblingly replied, 'Sioux.'"

The old Indian who narrated this story, was silent. He gazed upon the blazing fire; gave out a guttural sound, and then whiffing his pipe several times, continued:

"Nim-pe-wa-pa brave! Nim-pe-wa-pa no fear Sioux! Nim-pe-wa-pa's heart be big! Rousing the band, the Chippewas were soon in pursuit of the fleeing enemy, led by Nim-pe-wa-pa; but the wily savages had crossed the river, passed the boundary line, and could only be reached by confronting the whole Sioux nation; so, chafing for revenge the Chippewas returned to their camp on the silent shores of Me-de-wa-ka.

"It was night! The full-orbed moon sent a ray of mellow light down upon the beautiful lake, while on the shores of the sparkling water, numerous bands of Indians regaled themselves, either reclining upon the mossy banks or sailing in their light canoes over the limpid waves. The prattle and laughter of childhood; the ringing, gleeful notes of maidens; the plaintive songs of mothers, as they lulled their loved ones to sleep, gave a charm to the scene and presented a picture unrivaled in beauty and in innocence.

"The stars stooped down and kissed the fair maiden, He-le-o-pa, as with a soft tread and a light bound, she skipped among her companions the fairest of them all. With a perfect figure; beautiful, soft, black eyes; jet black hair, and clear complexion; with a merry laugh and a heart warm and generous in its impulses, no wonder she was the queen of her sex and the loved of her tribe. Just eighteen moons had passed over her fair head, and still so innocent, still so lovely, still so charming!"

The old Indian paused again, dropped his head upon his hands, uttered a moan, and then, as if recalling something in the long past, became as calm and as cold as marble, and continued his story:

"Up a short distance from the lake, embosomed in the arms of nature, nestling with the flowers, and listening to the whip-poor-will, wandered He-le-o-pa, all unmindful of the fright she had received but a short time before. The noise of the children had ceased; the moon was high in the blue sky; the quietness brooded over and about the lake; the Indians puffed their pipes, and recalled the stirring scenes of many a fight, when, all of a sudden, there was a piercing scream. It broke out again on the evening air, and the echo came back to remind the peaceful Indian village that an enemy was in their midst. The women and children entered their tepees, the men clutched their guns, and, hastening in the direction of the noise, halted. What means it? Who is missing?

"It seemed that while He-le-o-pa wandered in the moonlight, talking, as it were, with invisible beings, a company of thirty Sioux Indians stole in upon her, seized her, bound her to a pony, and were flying with her to the camp of the enemy. Before any concert of action could be devised by those who had congregated where the noise was heard, Nim-pe-wa-pa had mounted his steed, and, giving a most mournful wail, bounded in among them, and, screaming, 'He-le-o-pa, revenge and death!' dashed into the thicket, followed by his friends.

The old Indian paused again, when my interpreter asked—"Kan-e-de-ka, what then?" He refilled his pipe, then drawing himself up to his full height, exclaimed—"Nisisshin," which means good, and closed his story in the following graphic manner:

"Nim-pe-wa-pa's pony sped like an arrow! Through the bushes, over logs, jumping ravines, he seemed to possess the power of the incarnate. He, Nim-pe-wa-pa, rode the air and his men fled like birds at his command. The retreating Sioux are now in the distance, dimly seen in the moonlight. Ten of Nim-pe-wa-pa's men have left the main party to intercept them. On they rush, pell-mell! The Chippewas are gaining; the Sioux are scattering! With the impetuosity of a hurricane, Nim-pe-wa-pa darts down upon them! He approaches them, and in the full moonlight, fires! Mad with revenge, he continues the onslaught! He draws nearer; again he fires; a Sioux falls! How he gloats as he tears the scalp from his head, and then again continues the pursuit. In the meantime his friends have come up to the rescue, and soon begin one of the fiercest Indian battles on record. Hand to hand they meet; hand to hand they fall; hand to hand they die! Where is He-le-o-pa? Death! death! death!

"The party of ten Chippewas have intercepted the flying Sioux! They close in upon them! Red, gory blood curdles in the moonlight! Nim-pe-wa-pa rides like a demon! Five of the enemy have fallen from his unerring aim, and still, with loss of vital force from a dangerous wound, he continues the conflict! Dashing into the thickest of the fight, he makes one desperate effort, and in that effort he confronts the Indian who has He-le-o-pa bound to his horse, and with an impetuous plunge, dismounts him, but in the act, the animal upon which He-le-o-pa is secured, falls dead! Nim-pe-wa-pa reels, staggers, drops to the earth! The conflict is over! Several Chippewas and eight Sioux lie dead upon the field! Twenty-two of the enemy have escaped; three Chippewas are lifeless! The bodies of He-le-o-pa and Nim-pe-wa-pa are brought tenderly back to the lodge, and there, amid great lamentation, they repose side by side. All of a sudden there is great consternation in the camp! He-le-o-pa breathes! opens her eyes! moves! lives!—IS NOT DEAD!"

The old Indian arose from the camp-fire, strode back and forward for a few moments, and then mournfully added:

"They buried Nim-pe-wa-pa on a little knoll, overlooking Me-de-wa-ka, near the Ki-e-le-pa (or old tepee ground), and for fifty moons the faithful He-le-o-pa visited and planted flowers upon the grave of her noble, brave, and devoted lover."

Parties who visit the lake can see the spot where Nim-pe-wa-pa was buried, which is marked by a body of stones, placed there by the hands of the whole tribe, who revered the memory of the great and good Nim-pe-wa-pa. I should also add, that a part of the old Indian village, where Nim pe-wa-pa and He-le-o-pa lived, and where the former was killed, is now embraced in what is known as Central Park, where the shores slope down gradually to the lake, and where the land is thickly studded with trees. It is a quiet and sequestered spot, and, as one wanders over the knolls and in the valleys, shadowed by thick foliage, in imagination he can hear the sweet spirit voice of He-le-o-pa mournfully wailing for the loss of her lamented lover.

THE MISSISSIPPI RIVER AND ITS SCENERY.

THE INFANT RIVER ONLY SEVEN INCHES ACROSS IT.

THIS great river, upon whose broad and capacious bosom millions of bushels of wheat will yet float to the Gulf and from thence to Europe, and whose almost entire surface in a few succeeding years, will be dotted with steamboats unsurpassed for beauty and excellence, as many of the boats now are, is, in a straight line, measuring from its source, Lake Itasca — to its mouth, the Gulf of Mexico—eleven hundred and sixty-four miles. By the channel of the river it is two thousand, eight hundred miles in length. The population contiguous to the Mississippi river, will exceed 24,000,000, or nearly half of the population of the United States, and in ten years, with the present increase of emigration, the population in the valley and beyond, will reach 30,000,000, or a preponderance of power in the American nation. There are about one hundred cities and towns on the river from St. Paul to St. Louis; about eight above St. Paul, and about one hundred and fifty below St. Louis to the Gulf, making in all, two hundred and fifty-eight cities and towns on the river from its source to its mouth. This great valley of the Mississippi contains 768,000,000 acres of the finest lands in the world, sufficient to make more than one hundred and fifty states as large as Massachusetts. It embraces more territory than Great Britain, France,

Spain, Austria, European Turkey and Italy combined. If peopled as thickly as Massachusetts, it would contain four times the present population of the United States; if as populous as France, it would hold as many as now inhabit the whole of Europe.

H L. Gordon, in his Legends of the Northwest, sweetly sings:

"Onward rolls the Royal River, proudly sweeping to the sea,
Dark and deep and grand, forever wrapt in myth and mystery.
Lo, he laughs along the highlands, leaping o'er the granite walls;
Lo, he sleeps among the islands, where the loon her lover calls.
Still, like some huge monster winding downward through the prairied plains,
Seeking rest but never finding, till the tropic gulf he gains.
In his mighty arms he claspeth now an empire broad and grand;
In his left hand lo he graspeth leagues of fern and forest land;
In his right the mighty mountains, hoary with eternal snow,
Where a thousand foaming fountains singing seek the plains below.
Fields of corn and feet of cities, lo the mighty river laves,
Where the Saxon sings his ditties o'er the swarthy warriors' graves."

The first boat to ascend the Mississippi river, was the Virginia, in May, 1823, or sixty-one years ago. She was a stern-wheeler—length 118x24. Now the fleet of boats from St. Louis, owned by two companies, number twenty daily, and among them are several which will easily accommodate five hundred passengers. The Virginia might have cost $15,000; one of the present boats alone cost $40,000, and the whole amount invested in the Mississippi steamboat trade, will reach $2,000,000, and everything indicates a vast increase of trade upon this immense river, which, sooner or later, must become the thoroughfare for western grain to the seacoast and to Europe.

Contemplating the past and realizing the present, I

can appreciate Mr. Gordon's further allusion to the Mississippi, when he says:

"On thy bosom, Royal River, silent sped the birch canoe,
Bearing brave with bow and quiver, on his way to war or woo;
NOW with flaunting flags and streamers—mighty monsters of the deep,
Lo the puffing, panting steamers, through the foaming waters sweep;
And behold the grain-fields golden, where the bison grazed of eld,
See the fanes of forests olden by the ruthless Saxon felled,—
Plumed pines that spread their shadows ere Columbus spread his sails,
Firs that fringed the mossy meadows ere the Mayflower braved the gales;
Iron oaks that nourished bruin, while the Vikings roamed the main,
Crashing fall in broken ruin for the greedy marts of gain."

Recent information would indicate that the Mississippi river has its source from another lake than that of Itasca, and which is alleged to be much larger and handsomer than the historical sheet of water which, for so many years has been claimed to be the source of the great Father of Waters.

The first white man who ever saw Lake Itasca, was Schoolcraft, in the year 1832. Some twenty years later a party of explorers visited the lake, who describe it as a three-pointed star, and out of some eight thousand lakes in Minnesota, in shape, there is not another one like it. Within about two and a half miles of the lake can be seen a little rill of water meandering through the marsh, and this little rivulet, measuring only

SEVEN INCHES ACROSS IT,

is the infant Mississippi, and the little lake, only a mile long and not so wide, is where the first drop of water in the river comes from. It is now claimed that two other lakes exist above Itasca, and that the furthermost one is the real source of the Mississippi, but time and research will be necessary to establish this assertion beyond a doubt.

The scenery on the Mississippi river equals anything the traveler finds in Europe. The many points, bays, promontories, bluffs, canyons, prairies and beautiful landscapes which meet the eye, afford a never-ceasing source of pleasure, and the tourist on the boat, being free from dust and the jostle of the cars, enjoys serenely the bracing air, as it invigorates his lungs, or plays with his hair, or cools his fevered brow, while the palace steamer plows her way northward, or descends southward, riding the water like a thing of life. Millions of dollars will yet be expended in improving this great thoroughfare, which will drain a vast empire beyond of its wealth, bring into existence thousands of miles of railroads, and build up a city at the head of navigation, unequaled in population and in wealth by any metropolis in the West. And then, for ages and ages, as in the past so in the future, the Mississippi will continue its ceaseless flow, murmuring its lullaby dirge over thousands of those who, to-day, mingle in the great throng of our busy life, but whose memories will be washed away by the waves of the great river as they dash against the shores and obliterate the land marks of time.

"Faintly flow, thou falling river,
Like a dream that dies away,
Down to ocean gliding ever,
Keep thy calm, unruffled way.
Time, with such a silent motion,
Floats along on wings of air,
To eternity's dark ocean,
Burying all its treasures there."

THE BATTLE FOR THE APRON.

VARIOUS tribes of Indians have various modes of punishments for the various violations of their laws; but it is only among the Indians of the far West where it is left for the women of the tribe to punish the males for certain injuries received. Perhaps it would be a good idea to introduce this custom among the whites, in which case unprincipled men would be brought to feel the full force of injured innocence, and society would be greatly benefited even by the introduction of new ideas more radical than our own, respecting the punishment of men for a crime, which needs only the Indian mode of treatment to effect a positive cure. Let us admit that we can learn something even from the savages. A writer for the New York Sun, pens the following as occuring at Poplar river, Montana, among a tribe of Indians known as the Yanktonais:

"Recently there was witnessed here one of the most singular scenes of Indian life—the punishment by four Indian girls, the daughters of Polecat, of a young Indian hunter who had assaulted one of their number." The following description is that of an eye witness:

"The tribe forms a huge ring in which the savage who provoked the animosity of the Polecat family, is summarily thrust. He looks sullen and dogged. He has a hard fight before him, and he knows it; but he is a man of his hands, and he means to wear those girls out if it lies in his muscle and prompt and effectual work. He may strike them anywhere above the breast, and kill them, if a blow in the neck will do it, but bullets and arrows are ready for him if he strikes foul. The girls, on the other hand, must take off his apron. If they accomplish that, he is disgraced to the uttermost moment of his life, driven from his tribe, left to starve on the prairie, and all Indians cautioned against harboring, feeding or associating with him. The injured woman is allowed to have such squaws as she may select to assist her. But, if she chooses too many to effect her purpose, it is a disgrace to her; and so she is careful to select only enough to make the battle nearly equal.

"The Polecat girls are the belles of the Yanktonais tribe. If a squaw can be pretty, these girls are beautiful; and, by virtue of their attractions and their fathers' possessions in horses and other satisfactory property, they are the aristocrats of the camp. Perhaps for that reason they ask no help in their present undertaking; and for that reason also, perhaps, their savage sisters giggle and exchange whispers as the four girls step into the ring and approach the waiting buck. All five are in full war-paint. Down the hunter's cheeks and along his neck are alternate sepia and green and yellow stripes on a background of brilliant red, while his chest, sides and back are tricked out with rude pictures of guns, bows and horses. The girls have smeared their faces with a coating of red, over which lies another of green, striped with yellow. Their hair is unfastened at the back, and the front locks are braided with otter fur. Each wears a skirt and leggings; but their blankets are laid aside, and their muscular brown arms are displayed.

"There are no preliminaries. The girls dash at their

enemy and attempt to grasp him. If all hands manage to get hold of him, half the battle is accomplished. But he meets them squarely and fairly, planting a cruel blow between the eyes of the girl he had injured, knowing that if she is finished he can compel her to call off the rest. She is the general of the attacking forces and the prime object of attack. Over she goes like a pin-wheel; but she is up again, her face streaming with blood and her eyes swelling. The elder girl has contrived to secure a waisthold, and locked her hands behind his back. His fists fall upon her upturned face with frightful force; but she keeps her hold. The two other girls are pressing him hard from behind, but his elbows work like battering-rams, and one steps back with her hands pressed tightly to her breast and a look of agony in her eyes. Now he whirls suddenly, planting ponderous blows upon the face and head of the girl who on her knees still clings to his waist with a death-grip. He fairly raises her from the ground as he spins, but her hold never relaxes.

"His earlier victim again dashed at him, and is rewarded by a crashing stroke on the mouth. She reels, but recovers and darts again to receive his fist on her neck with a force that whirls her half a dozen paces off and drops her like a log. Not a word is spoken. The thud of his fists, and the heavy breathing of the struggling contestants, are the only sounds. The last rally of the prostrate girl has enabled the rear party to catch the buck, and one has twined her arms around his neck, while the other hangs to his wrist. His left hand is still free, and it fairly twinkles in the air as he batters the maiden at his waist. Her grasp is like iron, but her head reels and sways as his heavy hand falls on it with a noise that reaches the farthest side of the irregular ring. Her eyes are closed and her breath comes convulsively. Were the fourth girl there to grasp that arm, the fight would soon end.

"The girl behind is choking him, and he employs new tactics. Grasping the kneeling girl by the throat, he pounds the face of the one behind him with the back of his head. No vanity prompts her to let him go. She tightens her grip and buries her face in the back of his neck. The fourth girl is up, staggering and dazed. Brushing the blood from her eyes with an angry motion she approaches him, crouching as she moves. If the blow he has in store for her reaches the mark he will have another chance—for the girl at his waist is growing faint, and he can easily dispose of the other two. She comes at him like a cougar. The blow is delivered full upon her breast; but she grasps his wrist and writhes up his arm.

"Now he is beset with danger. The two at his arms and the one at his waist pull him forward; the girl behind, still strangling him, throws her weight on his back. In vain he attempts to straighten. The kneeling girl bends in her despairing struggle until her hair hangs on the ground. The other three show the muscles rigid in their arms as they press him down upon their kneeling sister. Suddenly he springs backward with a marvelous effort of strength. The fainting girl at his waist finds her hands torn apart. But that triumph was his defeat. With a crash he comes to the ground, three girls upon him. One plants herself on his face, and the other two kneel on his arms. There is a struggle, and then the youngest rises with a wild yell, waving the apron in her hand. Her yell is echoed by a low moan, as the mother of the prostrate hunter staggers out of the circle, and by a grunt of satisfaction, as Polecat recognizes the victory of his girls.

"To-morrow, somewhere up the river, that disgraced buck will be found with a bullet in his brain. Down in Chief Polecat's lodge four bruised and weary girls are mending each other's wounds with sisterly solicitude, and at the outer edge of the camp a bent old woman looks wistfully away to the North, where the shadows have swallowed up the form of the disgraced warrior."

A WHITE QUEEN.

HOLE-IN-THE-DAY, a noted Chippewa chief, already alluded to in these pages, when on a visit to Washington, fell in love with one of the servant girls at a hotel—I think the National—and on proposing, in regular white man's style, he was accepted and the two lovers were married. The white wife returned West with the chief and was duly installed queen of the tepee at his home, which act aroused the ill-will of his several squaws, and soon after, as Hole-in-the-Day was riding along the road leading to his dwelling, he was assassinated and killed; and thus ended the career of one of the most celebrated Chippewa warriors who ever held power over an Indian tribe. Soon after the death of her husband, the white queen abandoned the Indian mode of living, and for aught we know, may have married again, and probably has, but history will give her the credit of being the only white Indian queen who was ever elevated to an Indian throne—such as it was—and that is fame enough for any ambitious girl, either American or Irish.

AN INDIAN'S THEORY OF THE CELESTIAL BODIES.

HAN-YE-TU-WE (NIGHT SUN), AN-PE-TU-WE (DAY SUN), AND THE STARS, WHO ARE THEIR CHILDREN.

THE Indians have a very peculiar idea of the heavenly bodies, and the theory they advance has in it, to the unsophisticated mind, a good deal of common sense and some reason. Of course a person of intelligence rejects their ideas, knowing them to be erroneous, and yet, the untutored savage, drawing his notions from nature, reasons out a very plausible and a very satisfactory solution—to them—of the heavenly visitants as they come and go in their seasons and startle them with their changes. Every tribe has its great man who gives these subjects his especial study, and the common Indian receives them as emanations from the Great Spirit.

H. L. Gordon, in his interesting work, says:

"Wa-zi-ya, pronounced Wah-zee-yah, is the god of the North or winter; a fabled spirit who dwells in the frozen North in a great tepee of ice and snow. From his mouth and nostrils he blows the cold blasts of winter. He and I-to-ka-go Wi-cas-ta—the spirit or god of the South, literally the south man—are inveterate enemies and always on the war-path against each other. In winter Wa-zi-ya advances southward and drives I-to-ka-go before him to the summer island; but in spring the god of the South, having renewed his youth and strength in the happy hunting grounds, is able to drive Wa-zi-ya back again to his icy wigwam in the North. Some Dakotas say that the numerous granite boulders scattered over the prairies of the West, were hurled in battle by Wi-zi-ya from his home in the North, at I-to-ka-go Wi-cas-ta.

"He-o-ka is one of the principal Dakota deities. He is a giant, but can change himself into a buffalo, a bear, a fish, or a bird. He is called the anti-national god or spirit. In summer he shivers with cold; in winter he suffers from heat; he cries when he laughs and he laughs when he cries. He is the reverse of nature in all things. He-o-ka is universally feared and revered by the Dakotas.

"All Northern Indians consider the East a mysterious and sacred land whence comes the sun. Their name for the East, is Wee-yo-hee-yan-pa, the sunrise. The Chippewas call it Waub-o-nong—the white land, or land of light, and they have many myths, legends and traditions relating thereto.

"The Dakotas believe that the Aurora Borealis is an evil omen and the threatening of an evil spirit—perhaps Wi-zi-ya, the winter god—some say a witch, or a very ugly old woman! When the lights appear, danger threatens and the warriors shoots at and often slay the evil spirit, but it rises from the dead again."

Most Indians believe that the stars are the spirits of their departed friends; that thunder is produced by the flapping of the wings of an immense bird; that the milky way is the bridge of stars that spans the vast sea of the sky, and the sun and moon walk over on it.

Mr. Riggs, in his "Tah-hoo Wa-kan," says, "that the

Indians believe that the sun and moon are twin brothers, but that An-pe-tu-wee—the sun—is the more powerful. The moon receives its power from his brother and obeys him. He watches over the earth when the sun sleeps. The Dakotas believe that the sun is the father of life. Unlike the most of their gods, he is beneficent and kind; yet they worship him in the most dreadful manner."

Other tribes of Indians have similar beliefs, among which are the Piutes, and this brings us to the legend of the celestial bodies, as narrated by an old Piute medicine man, who, being called upon to express his opinion of a moving comet, filled his pipe, stirred up the embers of a smoldering fire, and in broken English, said:

"The sun rules the heaven. He is the big chief; the moon is his wife and the stars are his children. The sun he eat him children whenever he can them catch. They are all the time afraid when he is passing through the above. When he, their father, the sun, gets up early in the morning, you see all the stars—his children—fly out of sight, go away into the blue, and they do not make to be seen again till he, their father, is about for going to bed—down deep under the ground—deep, deep, in a great hole. Here he go into this hole, and he crawl and he creep till he come to his bed; so then sleep there all the night. This hole is so little and he, the sun, is so big, that he cannot turn round in it, so he must, when he has had all his sleep, pass on then through, and we see him next morning come out in the East. When he so comes out, he begins to hunt up through the sky to catch and eat any that he can eat of the stars, his children. He, the sun, is not all seen; the shape of him is like a snake or a lizard. It is not his head that we can see, but his stomach stuffed with stars he has times and times devoured. His wife, the moon, she goes into the same hole as her husband, to sleep her naps. She has always great fear of him, the sun, that have her for his wife, and when he come into the hole to sleep, she long not stay there if he be cross.

"She, the moon, have great always fear of him, the sun, that have her for his wife, and when he come into the hole to sleeep, she long not stay there if he be cross. She, the moon, have great love for her children, the stars, and is happy to be traveling up where they are. And they, her children, feel safe, and smile as she passes along. But she, the mother, cannot help but that one must go every month. It is so ordered by Pah-ah, the Great Spirit, that lives above the place of all. Every month he do swallow one of his children. Then the mother moon feel sorrow. She must to mourn. Her face she do paint it black, for child is gone. But the dark you will see wear away from her face—little, little, little every day; after a time we see all the face bright of the mother moon. But soon he, the sun, her husband, swallow another child, and she put on again her face the pitch and the black."

"But how about the comet?" we inquired, to which he replied:

"Well, sometimes you see the sun snap at one of the stars, his children, and not get good, fast hold—only tear one hole and hurt it. It get wild of pain and go fly away across the sky with great spout of blood from it. It then very fraid, and as it fly, keep always its head turned to watch the sun, its father, and never turn away from him his face till he is far out of his reach."

The old Indian picked up his stick, wrapped his blanket about him, and was soon out of sight, leaving queer impressions of his peculiar theory.

THE INNER LIFE; OR, THE BEST PART OF THE INDIAN.

WHILE I have hitherto given, in my articles, one side of the Indian character, which is the brutal part of his nature, it would be wrong in me not to give the other side in as glowing colors as the facts will admit. The reader should remember that the Indian male child is taught in early life, to hunt, fish, kill, travel, roam from place to place, and to exist free from labor, as we view it, while the female child is drilled in the arduous duties of camp life; dressing and cooking the food, taking care of children, gathering and chopping wood, and performing all the menial duties incident to savage existence. The Indian who travels day after day in search of game, considers *that* labor, and this is so deemed by the squaws themselves, so that when the game comes into camp the women receive it, dress it, cook it, and thus the labor is equally divided between the males and females, who are called upon to provide for the necessities of growing families. What is particularly impressive to a white man, is the heavy burdens which are borne on the backs of the women, while the men carry nothing but their guns. And yet the men are kind to their wives and considerate to their children. Of course woman occupies an inferior position among the savages, and she gracefully submits to it as a law of their race. As one tribe of Indians is constantly preying upon and fighting another tribe, so, in self-defense, all the males are educated for war, in order that they may be able to protect their defenseless women and children from their enemy; and hence a warrior must spend his time in perfecting himself for battle, instead of demeaning himself by work.

Nothing presents a more pleasing or a more affectionate picture, than an Indian village on the banks of some loved lake, where all the social qualities of the savage are brought out in bold light. The men usually indulge in smoking and talking of their exploits in the field, while the old women sit about the smoldering embers of the tepee, and dwell in recounting exciting tales of the past, and the children gambol on the grassy slopes, or amuse themselves in their light canoes. There is a degree of tenderness shown in these scenes which is not visible generally to the casual observer, and hence, the inner life of the Indian is the best part of him.

It was a dark, stormy night in June, 1863, when I heard a most unearthly sound, resembling, somewhat the howlings of a dog, though more shrill and more doleful; and leaving my office, then located on the frontier, I strolled out over the deserted camp of our troops—just left for a campaign against the savages—and proceeding along in the darkness, followed the sound toward a friendly Indian lodge near by, where were the women and children of the scouts of the little army which was then on its way to chastise the Indians for their murderous deeds, committed the year before. Again came that horrible, thrilling sound, electrifying my system and raising my hair on my head, but I kept on in the direction from whence it emanated, until I ran against the bayonet of one of our guards and heard the sudden challenge—"Who goes there?"

In the excitement of the moment, I forgot where I was, but soon regaining consciousness, made myself known to the faithful soldier, passed the lines, penetrated the almost impenetrable darkness, entered a dingy tepee, and there confronted two squaws, one of whom held in her arms a bundle and was swaying to and fro over the slowly burning embers of a few sticks of half-consumed wood, and ever and anon sending up one of the most mournful sounds ever heard from a human throat. It swept out into the beating storm like the incoming of a great wave from the ocean, which, when it has reached a given point, breaks, and then subsides again into the element from whence it came. Starting in a low, gurgling sound, this "death wail" ascended gradually higher and higher, until at last it culminated in a shrill break of a female voice, and then, before the sound had entirely ceased, it was taken up again by the other squaw; and so, during that long and stormy night, came, and broke, and went, and came, and broke, and went again, above the raging, tossing, soughing winds, the moanings of that Indian mother, and her friend, over the little bones of the little child, encased in its little blanket that lay in its parent's arms. Above the raging elements I could hear the following sorrowful wail: (Translated from the Indian.)

"Swing, swing, little one, lullaby;
Thou'rt not left alone to weep;
Mother's cares for you—she is nigh;
Sleep, my little one, sweetly sleep;
Swing, swing, little one, lullaby;
Mother watches you—she is nigh;

Gently, gently, wee one, swing;
Gently, gently, while I sing,—
E-we-wa-wa-lullaby.
E-we-wa-wa-lullaby."

To-morrow would see it pass away from her sight forever! Her grief was simple, pure, deep, unaffected. Neither of these mourners noticed my intrusion, and so knowing that I could do them no good, I went out again into the darkness, threaded my way to, and passed the guard, sought my office and my couch, and dreamed all night of a golden-haired little girl whom I had left with her mother inside of the limits of civilization, and whose imaginative little prattle made me smile in my sleep as I dreamed of home, of loved ones, and of friends.

The Indians have a peculiar and very interesting custom of burying with their children, all their little trinkets and play-things, believing that they will want them in the happy hunting ground beyond the river of death. They also have a custom of so preserving the bodies of their children after death, that they will appear natural for some time, and when this naturalness has disappeared, and the skin becomes drawn down tighly over the features, then a night is set apart for the "death wail," and the next day the little one passes out of their sight, and with it, all its tiny, earthly possessions, wrapped up together, sometimes the body to be elevated in the air on poles, as protection against wild beasts, and sometimes to be buried in the earth beyond human vision forever!

The morning after the occurrence to which I have alluded, two lone Indian women moved out from their humble wigwam, carrying the bones of the dead child, and chanting a low, mournful sound, slowly wound up the hill on to the plateau, and in plain sight of the whole camp, deposited in the ground the body of their little darling, and then affectionately bending over the wee mound, and leaving food for the nourishment of the child on its journey, they kissed the soil, and wended their way back again to their lonely lodge, to no longer hear the patter of the little feet, or the music of the little voice, or the clasp of the little hand, or the touch of the little lip, but to feel an unutterable, incomprehensible void in the aching heart, as much so to the Indian mother as to that of the white.

A Mr. Farney, who has but recently returned from a visit among the Sioux, says that he never saw a jollier camp in his life than a Sioux village. The men sit in their tepees and smoke, and talk over their battles, and relate jokes that are received with unrestrained grunts and gurgles of laughter. The squaws are soft-voiced and graceful, and show a genuine mother love for their children. He met a squaw when out on a sketching tour with his Indian guide, who was running to fetch a medicine man, thirty miles away, to cure her sick baby. He told her to get into the wagon, and he would take her as far on her way as he was going, and he says the woman's grief was the most pathetic thing he ever saw. Her face was covered close with her blanket, and she sobbed and wept every moment of the way, nearly an hour's ride. The Indian Rachel refusing to be comforted, and the dusky girls singing softly in the moonlight, are what strike the artist's vision.

The Sioux pluck out every vestige of eyebrows and paint their faces a bright vermilion red and a ghastly yellow; they move without a sound of their moccasin-clad feet, and wrap their blankets about them so as to conceal their face, all but the brow and nose and a pair of luminous black eyes, rendered the more horrible by lack of eyebrows. Many of the beardless and full-featured braves have a certain serenity of manner that reminded the artist of nice old ladies. The old squaws, who bear the burdens of life, are horribly wrinkled and worn. A little girl, six years old, was arrayed for company in the following manner: She was painted a fine vermilion, daubed with yellow, and wore a cape studded with elk teeth, worth some hundreds of dollars.

He assisted at a Sioux musicale that would have delighted the society for the prevention of music. A young Indian of some quality sat in the center of the tepee with a big drum before him, on which he beat occasional discords. His young friends dropped in by twos and threes, and each hammered out his discord, smoked a pipe, took a cup of hot dog soup, and went his way. This thing was continued all the afternoon, and was a swell event in the village.

The outward, or exterior life of the Indian, is war, revenge, death, brutality, conquest! He is so educated from childhood. Traditionary history teaches him to never forget a wrong, especially on the part of another tribe, and these ideas are inculcated in the young, and so one generation after another possesses this blood-thirsty element. His inner, or domestic life, is different. It is seldom or ever we hear of wife-murder among the Indians, or of divorces, or wrangling in his family, although this sometimes does occur. To a great degree he lives and shares in common with his fellow Indians, is dependent one upon the other, and hence it is for his interest to be kind to his family and to his neighbors

Prior to the introduction of the customs of the whites among them, no nation was more victorious, and no peo ple have a stronger or a more settled belief in the existence of a Great Spirit, and in the hereafter, than the Indians. Aside from his war-like proclivities, which, as I have already said, come from his education, he is kind, generous, faithful to his word, brave, affectionate, truthful, and yet, lurking beneath all these, is a spirit of treachery, which seems to be a part of his existence. He draws his inspiration from nature and is therefore a child of nature; and if the whites had never wronged him, he would have been their best friend, as this is abundantly proven by the early history of these Indians when in a primitive state. His attachments are strong and his friendships lasting. Of course when war has been declared by the chiefs, all have to come under the rules of their mode of fighting, just as the people of the South sided with the Southern Confederacy; and while, therefore, some may be opposed to the indiscriminate slaughter and torture of the enemy, yet all must conform to the general rule; and yet, in the great massacre, in Minnesota, in 1862, Other-Day and Old Bets, and their companions, defied this rule at the risk of being killed, and very materially aided in saving the lives of a great many whites.

It is pleasant to contemplate, that for several years past, the Indians have been making rapid progress toward civilization, and in the next ten years it is fair to presume that they will become an agricultural and herding people with many of the accessories and some of the accomplishments of the whites, capable of self-government as a state by themselves. They are rapidly drifting toward that way. Apropos to this, I find the following paragraph in a late Western paper:

"Who will doubt that our Indians may be civilized? Young Hole-in-the-Day, son of the old Chippewa chief of that name, has, with a number of Indians from the White Earth reservation, been industriously working among the farmers in this vicinity during harvest. They bear the reputation of being good, steady laborers at binding, shocking, etc. And now, as we write, Hole-in-the-Day is doing the band-cutting for a threshing outfit, while the rest of the Indians are teaming and pitching equally well with the white men on the same job. Hole-in-the-Day has ten acres of wheat of his own at White Earth, and the others there have as high as twenty or twenty-five acres each, and their crops will, from all accounts, compare favorably with any in this section."

Hole-in-the-Day, the Chippewa chief, to whom frequent mention is made in these pages, was the father of the present young man to whom the above reference applies. A quarter of a century, even in the experience of the author, has made great and material changes in the character of the Indians of the Northwest, and everything indicates a more rapid advance to civilization in the future than in the past.

When the exterior life of the Indian has been outgrown, the interior man will develop, and this development will bring to the surface, a bright diamond, now hid amid the vast rubbish of decaying barbarism and unparalleled wickedness on the part of the whites.

AN-PE-TU-SA-PA.*

A LEGEND OF ST. ANTHONY FALLS.

VARIOUS writers on Indian history concede the fact that away back in the past, an Indian woman committed suicide with her children, by floating her canoe over the Falls of St. Anthony, and the legends seem to be well authenticated. Among the many accounts given of this tragical event, we find the statement of Shoot-from-the-Pine-Tree, an old Indian whose mother witnessed the scene, as the most truthful. It is told by Major Stephen H. Long, of the United States army, and is no doubt a true history of a painful event. The narrator says:

"A young Indian, of the Sioux nation, had espoused a wife, with whom he had lived happily for a few years, enjoying every comfort of which a savage life is susceptible. To crown the felicity of the happy couple, they had been blessed with two lovely children, on whom they doted with the utmost affection. During this time the young man, by dint of activity and perseverance, signalized himself in an eminent degree, as a hunter, having met with universal success in the chase. This circumstance contributed to raise him high in the estimation of his fellow savages and to draw a crowd of admirers about him, which operated as a spur to his ambition. At length some of his newly acquired friends, desirous of forming a connection which must

* Clouded Day. Ha! Ha! or Roaring, or Loud Laughing Water, is the Indian name for the Falls of St. Anthony.

operate greatly to their advantage, suggested the propriety of his taking another wife, as it would be impossible for one woman to manage his household affairs and wait upon all the guests his rising importance would call to visit him; that his importance to the nation was everywhere known and acknowledged, and that in all probability he would soon be called upon to preside as their chief. His vanity was fired at the thought; he yielded an easy compliance with their wishes, and accepted a wife they had already selected for him.

"After his second marriage, it became an object with him to take his new wife home and reconcile his first wife to the match, which he was desirous of accomplishing in the most delicate manner that circumstances would admit. For this purpose he returned to his first wife, who was yet ignorant of what had taken place, and by dissimulation attempted to beguile her into an approbation of the step he had taken. 'You know,' said he, 'I can love no one so much as I love you; yet I see that our connection subjects you to hardships and fatigue too great for you to endure. This grieves me much, but I know of only one remedy by which you can be relieved, and which, with your concurrence, shall be adopted. My friends, from all parts of the nation, come to visit me, and my house is constantly thronged by those who come to pay their respects, while you alone are under the necessity of laboring hard in order to cook their food and wait upon them. They are daily becoming more numerous, and your duties are becoming more arduous every day. You must be sensible that I am rising high in the esteem of the nation, and I have sufficient grounds to expect that I shall, before long, be a chief. These considerations have induced me to take another wife, but my affection for you has so far prevailed over my inclination in this respect, as to lead me to solicit your approbation before I adopt the measure. The wife I take shall be subject to your control in every respect, and will be always second to you in my affections.'

"She listened to his narrative with the utmost anxiety and concern, and endeavored to reclaim him from his purpose, refuting all the reasons and pretences his duplicity had urged in favor of it, by unanswerable arguments, the suggestions of unaffected love and conjugal affection. He left her, however, to meditate upon the subject, in hopes that she would at length give over her objections and consent to his wishes. She, in the meantime, redoubled her industry, and treated him invariably with more marked tenderness than she had done before; resolved to try every means in her power to dissuade him from the execution of his purpose. She still, however, found him bent upon it. She pleaded all the endearments of their former life, the regard had for the happiness of herself and the offspring of their mutual love, to prevail on him to relinguish the idea of taking another wife. She warned him of the fatal consequences that would result to their family upon his taking such a step. At length he was induced to communicate the event of his marriage. He then told her that a compliance on her part would be absolutely necessary; that if she could not receive his new wife as a friend and companion, she must admit her as a necessary incumbrance; at all events, they must live together. She was determined, however, not to remain the passive dupe of his hypocrisy. She took her two children, left his house and went to reside with her parents. Soon after she returned to her father's family, she joined them and others of her friends in an expedition up the Mississippi to spend the winter in hunting.

"In the spring, as they were returning laden with peltries, she and her children occupied a canoe by themselves. On arriving near the Falls of St. Anthony, she lingered by the way till the rest had all landed, a little above the chute. She then painted herself and her children, paddled her canoe immediately into the whirling eddy of the rapids, and commenced singing her death song, in which she recounted the happy scenes she had passed through, when she enjoyed the undivided affection of her husband, and the wretchedness in which she was involved by his inconstancy. In his interesting legends of the Northwest, the author gives this death song in the following lines:

'Mi-hi-hn-a ! * Mihihna ! my heart is stone;
The light has gone from my longing eyes;
The wounded loon in the lake alone
Her death-song sings to the moon and dies.

'Mihihna ! Mihihna ! the path is long,
The burden is heavy and hard to bear;
I sink—I die ! and my dying song
Is a song of joy to the false one's ear !

'Mihihna ! Mihihna ! my young heart flew
Far away with my brave to the bison chase;
To the battle it went with my warrior true,
And never returned till I saw his face.

'Mihihna ! Mihihna ! the boy I bore—
When the robin sang and my brave was true,
I can bear to look on his face no more,
For he looks, Mihihna, so much like you.

* Mee-heen-yah—My husband.

'Mihihna ! Mihihna ! the Scarlet Leaf
Has robbed my boy of his father's love;
He sleeps in my arms—he will find no grief
In the star-lit lodge in the land above.

'Mihihna ! Mihihna ! my heart is stone;
The light is gone from my longing eyes;
The wounded loon in the lake alone
Her death-song sings to the moon and dies."

"Her friends, alarmed at her situation, ran to the shore and begged her to paddle out of the current, while her parents, in the agonies of despair, rending their clothes and tearing out their hair, besought her to come to their arms. But all to no purpose; her wretchedness was complete, and must terminate only with her existence. She continued her course till she was borne headlong down the roaring cataract, and instantly dashed to pieces on the rocks below. No traces of either herself and her children, or the boat were ever found afterward. Her brothers, to be avenged of the the untimely fate of their sister, embraced the first opportunity and killed her husband, whom they considered the cause of her death, a custom sanctioned by the usage of the Indians, from time immemorial."

It is alleged that the spirit of An-pe-tu-sa-pa sits upon the island below the Falls, at night, and pours forth her sorrow in song; and it is also stated, with a considerable degree of certainty, that there are parties who, on moonlight evenings, can see the fated canoe, with the unfortunate mother and her innocent children, rushing swiftly along into the jaws of death.

MY LAST NIGHT IN A SIOUX INDIAN CAMP.

THE year following the great Indian massacre, wherein nearly one thousand innocent settlers lost their lives, Gen. Sibley was authorized to fit out an army of troops then ready for the South, and pursue the guilty savages and annihilate them, if possible, but at any rate, drive them into and across the Missouri river. The latter point he accomplished, and he was sagacious enough to see, that previous to starting out, it was essentially necessary to have Indian scouts to pilot his army over the trackless plains and detect the movements of the enemy; so he chose from those savages then at his command, such a number as he could trust, and in order to secure good faith on their part, they agreed to leave their women and children in his possession as hostages, during their absence. The camp of these friendly Indians was located several miles from our own, for various reasons, among which were, that they would be removed from the viciousness of the soldiers, and would act as an outlying or alarming post to the main camp. The only man among these friendly Indians, was a fat, pussy half-breed, by the name of Le Rock, who had general charge of their wants, and as none of the soldiers had permission to enter the Indian line, of course they were as secluded as though a thousand miles away. My duties as Commissary and Quartermaster, brought me in daily contact with these Indians, and I had, therefore, more favorable opportunities for observation than others; and to their credit, let me say, I never had occasion to find fault with any of their acts. The women used to come into my office, and by way of banter, call me "squaw foot," a name they gave me in consequence of the smallness of my feet; but they were never troublesome, never meddlesome, never impudent.

An Indian girl is the very essence of timidity, and this is especially so, if she is beautiful, and when confronting a white man, she will cringe and dodge and peep from behind her mother, and even blush as the eye of the spectator is fixed upon her. The older women were modest and retiring, and I never knew one to enter my office unless invited, which, I must confess, was an exception to a general rule in Indian character, for they usually bob in and out, when and where they please. Perhaps the fact that I fed these Indians, and that they received full and good rations, led them to suppose I was "Wa-kon," or sacred, for they well knew, from actual experience, that the general run of Government officers was to steal from them all they could. Be this as it may, they entertained the highest regard for me, and I can only account for it on the ground that I dealt fairly and justly by them.

The rush, the bustle, and the excitement of the camp, had come and gone! Three thousand soldiers were trudging over the plains in search of the savages, while only a few men were left to guard the fort; and then, after several weeks, came the order to "vacate," and myself and brother officers began picking up the odds and ends of the camp, preparatory to a stampede toward civilization. While in the midst of this duty, appeared Le Rock, who, having heard of our contemplated moving, came to invite me to spend the last night of my frontier duty in his tepee. Indeed, he conveyed the gratifying intelligence that the whole Indian outfit had extended the invitation; and so, reasoning that probably this would be my last opportunity to mingle with the uncouth, yet kindly-hearted red people—and time has demonstrated the correctness of my conclusions—I consented to go.

The afternoon of the evening before we broke camp was beautiful. I buckled on two loaded pistols, slipped a large knife into my belt, and, calling for my favorite horse, mounted and turned his head in the direction of the Indian camp. Nothing was more lovely than the scene that met my view. Stretching off for five or six miles was the Yellow Medicine valley, and from the top of the hills that lined it on either side the landscape was of a most charming character. I now was on ground but lately traversed by Indian war-parties; on ground where sickening scenes had transpired; on ground owned by the Indians; and on ground but recently the home of Little Crow, the great Sioux chief, who had instigated the war. On the brow of a hill to the left, in imagination, I could see the family of Joe Reynolds fleeing from the infuriated savages; could hear the screams of the females, as the red devils made hot pursuit; could hear the crushing of the tomahawks into the skulls of two of the women; could see the struggling Miss Williams, trying to get free from a fate worse than death; could almost feel the presence of the enemy at my side. My courage failed me, and I turned back; and yet, how beautiful! how still! how grand! Nature never looked more charming, more inviting, more lovely. "No," I soliloquized,

"I will go ahead; it is my last chance, and if I fall by the bullets of some Indian spy, who may be lurking in the neighborhood, my wish is to die at once; not by a lingering death of torture; and then, plucking up courage, I turned my horse's head, and was soon on a brisk canter up the valley.

Arriving at the camp, the first to greet me were about fifty dogs, whose furious barking was echoed back from the hills; then followed the imposing figure of Le Rock; then fifty newly-painted female faces, with large, luminous black eyes, peeping out from under shawls and blankets, and tepees; and the low giggle and soft voice announced my coming. Le Rock treated me with great cordiality, and the women would look down on the ground and laugh at my feet. There might have been some twenty-five tepees in all, located near the edge of a forest and contiguous to water, but with no rule as to regularity. I was conducted to each one of these tepees and formally introduced, and then, later in the evening, was invited to a singing-school, at which all the women were present, except those either unwell, or detained at home by sickness in the family. This singing-school was an imposing scene in Indian life, and was intended to show me how the Indians were progressing in civilization, for during the evening "Mary, to the Savior's Tomb," "Old Hundred," and other familiar religious hymns, translated into the Indian language, were sung by the girls, and apparently greatly enjoyed by them. Then followed an address by myself, in which I recapitulated the pleasures I experienced in attending singing-school in New England, and going home with the girls, coupled by complimentary allusions to their excellent behavior and the rapid progress they had made. A good many eyes sparkled, a good many lips smiled, a good many ears tingled, and a good many cheeks blushed when the interpreter conveyed to my hearers what I had been saying; and altogether it was an enjoyable evening, for I had forgotten that the husbands and fathers of these very people had been engaged in the massacre of the whites the year before; had forgotten the peculiar feelings in the afternoon as I rode to their camp; had forgotten the dangerous position I was then in, when only a few savages could have killed us all; forgotten that I had yet a night to pass through before morning would put me inside of the circle of safety. I consoled myself, however, with the thought that whatever might happen it was of my own choosing, and what was to be would be.

At about eleven o'clock Le Rock escorted me to his "grand" lodge which differed from the others only in size, and pointing to the post of "honor"—opposite to the entrance—directed my eye to a feather bed, with pillow-cases, sheets, etc. In the center of the tepee was a poor apology for a fire, while on the right was the bed of an old woman—a widow and her child—and on the left was the inviting couch of my entertainer, which consisted of an old Buffalo robe, a soiled pair of blankets, and a greasy pillow. My bed had belonged to one of the unfortunate white settlers who had fallen a victim to savage revenge, and had been carefully manipulated for my use. As it was a very warm evening in June, and as I had a strap buckled about my body, in which were two heavy pistols, and there was a fire in the tepee, the outlook for a cool and refreshing sleep, was anything but pleasant; in addition to which,

I was determined that my pistols should never leave my side, and consequently could not disrobe, so that, after I had thrown myself upon the feather bed and swallowed a half-dozen whiffs of smoke, which was driven down into the lodge, I began to sweat and to mentally swear over the awful plight I was in, and yet I could not abuse the hospitality of one who had been so kind. Le Rock bundled in with his squaw—a poor, half-frightened-to-death, over-worked creature—and in one minute was in a sound sleep, his heavy breathings being like the swells of the ocean; and when he got fully under way, his snoring absolutely shook the lodge pole and dispelled all sleep from my thoughts.

And there I lay, sweating, and thinking and listening, the smoke making the water run from my eyes, and the noise outside forcing me to imagine that the hostile Indians were about to make an attack upon the camp, until, all of a sudden, about twelve o'clock, the woman on my left shot up as straight as though pulled by a string, crossed her limbs, took her pipe, gave several puffs, uttered a grunt, and instantly the son followed the example of his mother. Passing the pipe to the lad, the old squaw arose, stirred up the dying embers, filled the tepee full of smoke, put on a huge iron pot, and gathering up a double-handful of the entrails of an ox, given to them the day before, placed them in the pot, filled it with water and began stirring for the evening meal. "Good Heavens," I said to myself mentally, "can this be for me? How shall I elude this terrible catastrophe?" And while thus devising some means to escape the ordeal, up came Le Rock like an arrow, who seized the pipe, gave a puff and immediately after followed his wife, going through with the same antics.

And then the water in the pot bubbled and boiled and the old woman stirred in the dirt and more smoke swept down upon my unfortunate head and the sweat poured off me in great drops, but I had made up my mind what to do—*I would never touch that dish*—and if invited to do so, I would be sound asleep, "just as sure as shooting!"

True enough, Le Rock approached my bed, shook me—I was lost in the arms of Morpheus—but, finally came to consciousness, plead sickness, was very sorry, etc., and at last was permitted to go on with my pleasurable sweating, while my companions "waded in," and disposed of the contents of that six quart pot, inside of thirty minutes; and then, tumbling over like logs into their beds, snored until morning. I can truthfully say, I never passed a more terrible night in my life than on this occasion, not that the Indians were to blame—for it was their modes, their habits, their customs—but I could not conform to them. Had I divested myself of all fear in the first place, settled my mind that all was right in the second place, partook of their food in the third place, smoked their pipe in the fourth place—as most men would have done—it is quite likely I should have passed a pleasant time, but memory now only recalls one of the most horrible nights—and I am glad it was the last—that I ever spent in a Sioux Indian camp.

PECULIAR INDIAN TRADITIONS.

THEIR BELIEF IN THE SUPERNATURAL — ALL SORTS OF SPIRITS THAT ROAM EVERYWHERE — SPIRITUAL MEDIUMS.

ONE who is familiar with Indian history cannot but be impressed with the universal belief that prevails among all the savage tribes of the existence of spirits that dwell everywhere, and roam throughout the domain of this material world; nor can he forget that they have an abiding faith in a future, which they term the "happy hunting ground." They say that the "bridge of souls" leads from the earth, over dark and stormy waters, to the spirit land. The Indian deity is supposed to be invisible, yet everywhere present; he is an avenger and searcher of hearts. They also aver that the Indian has three souls, and that after death that which has done well goes to the warm country, that which has done evil goes to the cold region, and that the other guards the body. When a Dakota is sick he thinks the spirit of an enemy or some animal has entered into his body, and the principal business of the "medicine man" is to cast out the unclean spirit with incantations and charms. Nearly all the Dakotas believe in witches and witchcraft; and they hold that the "milky way" in the heavens is the pathway of the spirits; and also believe that over this pathway the spirits of the dead pass to the spirit land.

Unk-te-hee is the Great Spirit of all, who created the earth and man, and who formerly dwelt in a vast cavern under the Falls of St. Anthony, which, they believed, were in the center of the earth, and from which a path led to the great beyond. This Deity sometimes reveals himself in the form of a huge buffalo bull. From him proceed invisible influences. Previous to forming the earth, he assembled in grand conclave, all the aquatic tribes, and ordered them to bring up dirt from beneath the waters, proclaiming death to the disobedient. The beaver and otter forfeited their lives. At last the muskrat went beneath the water, and, after a long time, appeared at the surface, nearly exhausted, with some dirt. From this Unk-te-hee fashioned the earth into a large circular plane. The earth being finished, he took a deity, one of his own offspring, and grinding him to powder, sprinkled it upon the earth, and this produced many worms. The worms were then collected and scattered again. They matured into infants, and these were then collected and scattered and became full-grown Dakotas.

Some hold to the theory that the evil or bad spirit is what is called a Thunder Bird, while others, that it is a great black spider, which inhabits fens and marshes, and lies in wait for his prey. At night he often lights a torch —evidently the jack-o-lantern—and swings it on the marshes to decoy the unwary into his toils. The Great Unk-te-hee and the Great Thunder Bird, or Great Spider, had a terrible battle to determine which should be the ruler of the world, but Unk-te-hee conquered.

Carver's cave was called by the Dakotas, "Wa-kan-Tepee"—sacred lodge. In his book of travels, Carver says: "It is a remarkable cave, of an amazing depth. The Indians term it 'Wakan tepee,' that is, the 'dwelling of the Great Spirit.' It is now the receptacle for lager beer."

A beautiful belief is, that the stars are the spirits of their departed friends, and that meteors are messengers from the land of spirits, warning off impending danger; that the evening star is the Virgin Star, and is the spirit of the Virgin wrongfully accused at the feast.

The sun they consider the Father; so they believe the earth to be the mother of all life. The Indian swears by the Father as—"An-pe-tu-wee—hear me; this is true." They also pray thus: "Wa-kan! Ate, on-she-ma-da! Sacred Spirit—Father! have mercy upon me!"

Toon-Kan, or Inyan, is the stone idol or god of the Dakotas. This god dwells in stone and in rock, and is, they say, the oldest god of all—grandfather of all living things. Some writers think, and with considerable reason, that the stone is merely the symbol of the everlasting, all pervading, invisible Ta-koo-wa-kan—the essence of all life—pervading all nature, animate and inanimate. Rev. Mr. Riggs, says:

"The religious faith of the Dakotas is not in his god as such. It is an intangible, mysterious something of which they are only the embodiment, and that in such measure and degree as may accord with the individual fancy of the worshiper. Each one will worship some of these divinities, or neglect, or despise others, but the great object of all their worship, whatever its chosen medium, is the Ta-koo Wa-kan, which is the supernatural and mysterious. It comprehends all mystery, secret power and divinity. Awe and reverence are its due, and it is as unlimited in manifestation as it is in ideas. All life is Wa-kan; so, also, is everything which exhibits power, whether in action as the winds and drifting clouds, or in passive endurance, as the boulder by the wayside. For even the commonest stick and stones have a spiritual essence, which must be reverenced as a manifestation of the all-pervading, mysterious power that fills the universe."

God, in the Dakota tongue is Wa-kan Tan-ka, which means, Big Spirit, or the Big Mysterious. The medicine men claim to be aided by unseen spirits, and hence are called—"men supernatural." They assert they are the sons or disciples of Unk-te-hee. The sacred O-zu-ha, or medicine sack, must be made of the skin of the otter, the coon, the weasel, the squirrel, a certain kind of fish, or the skin of serpents. It must contain four kinds of medicine (or magic), representing birds, beasts, herbs and trees, viz:—The down of the female swan, colored red, the roots of certain grasses, bark from the roots of cedar trees, and hair of the Buffalo. From this combination proceeds a Wa-kan influence, so powerful that no human being, unassisted, can resist it. Mr. Riggs says: "By great shrewdness, untiring industry, and *more or less of actual demonical possession*, they convince great numbers of their fellows, and, in the process are convinced themselves, of their sacred character and office."

The Good or Great Spirit is called "Mi-cha-bo." "In autumn, in the moon of the falling leaf, ere he composes himself for his winter's sleep, he fills his great pipe and takes a god-like smoke. The balmy clouds from his pipe float over the hills and woodlands, filling the air with the haze of Indian summer." The Jossakeeds are soothsayers, who are able, by the aid of spirits, to read the past as well as the future.

"Ka-be-bon-ik-ka" is the god of storms, thunder, lightning, etc. By his magic, the giant that lies on the mountain was turned to stone. He always gives warnings before he finally sends the severe cold of winter, in order that all creatures may have time to prepare for it. There are also water spirits, that dwell in caverns in the depths of the lake, and in some respects resemble the Unk-te-hee of the Dakota. This is a Chippewa spirit.

It is somewhat remarkable, that nearly every spiritual medium in this country and in Europe, claims that he or she is guided by an invisible Indian chief, and that the so-called human forms that are materialized in spiritual circles, are produced by Indian spirits. The reasons assigned for this are, that the Indian, being more closely allied to nature than to any other race, and believing in the spiritual theory, having never been hampered with religious bigotry, as are the whites, have less to overcome when they pass away, and have greater power to return at the option of their will. This idea I have woven into my Indian legend called "Min-ne-too-ka," and by perusing it the reader will get a very correct idea of the spiritual belief that pertains to all Indian tribes, no matter how savage their natures, or how domesticated their tastes.

Major James W. Lynd, in his MS. history of the Dakotas, in the Minnesota Historical Society, says:

"The belief in the powers of some of the Dakotas to call up and converse with the spirits of the dead, is strong, though not general. They frequently make feasts to their spirits and elicit information from them, of distant relatives or friends. Assembling at night in a lodge, they smoke, put out the fire, and then drawing their blankets over their heads, remain singing in unison, in a low key, until the spirit gives them a picture. This they pretend the spirit does, and many a hair-erecting tale is told of spirits' power to reveal hidden things and to communicate unknown facts.

"In 1830 a war-party of Sioux went in search of the Chippewas, and those left at home became anxious for their return, when an old woman, ninety years of age, said she would consult the spirits; so a lodge was cleared, a small fire kindled, and the old woman entered, closing the door after her tightly. Seating herself she lighted the black pipe, and after smoking for a time, laid it aside, beat out the fire, and then drawing her blanket over her head, she commenced to sing in a low key, in anticipation of revelations from the spirits. Crowds of women and children, with a few old men, surrounded the lodge, awaiting anxiously for what should happen. Suddenly the old woman was heard to cry out as if in extreme terror, and hastily throwing open the door they found her lying upon the ground in a swoon. On coming to, she related that she had a terrible picture. Fourteen men rose up from the west, bloody and without their scalps, and thirteen rose up up from the east with blood upon their forms, and were in the act of falling. This referred to the advanced body of the Sioux that had gone ahead. Four days after this revelation the Sioux came home with fourteen scalps, but with thirteen of their own party on biers, which confirmed the old woman's statement in every respect. 'Certain men also profess to have an unusual amount of the Wa-kan, or divine principle in them. By it they assume to work miracles, laying on of hands, curing the sick, etc., and many more wonderful operations. Some of them pretend to recollect a former state of existence, even naming the particular body they formerly lived in. Others again, assert a power over nature, and their faculty of seeing into futurity and of conversing with the deities.' "

The Arabs believe that when a man rises up from sleep in the morning, the spirit of God sits upon his right shoulder, and the Devil on his left. A Turi-Arab, therefore, on awaking, invariably repeats the exercising formula: "I seek refuge in God from Satan accursed with stones," sprinkling himself, when possible, with water, as he utters the words. Without this precaution they believe the good spirit would take flight and the evil one would remain with them throughout the day. At sunset the same ceremony is repeated.

For some information contained in this article, outside of my own knowledge, I am indebted to H. L. Gordon, Revs. Riggs, Neil and Pond, all of whom are excellently well posted on Indian history, and are the very best authorities from whom I could quote as to the beliefs and peculiar traditions of the Indians of the Northwest.

An old soldier, whose name I cannot obtain, gives to the press some interesting information that was conveyed to him by the celebrated Indian Missionary, Father De Smet, who for years mingled with the Indians on the Missouri river, and who was among the very first in the country to discover gold in the Black Hills—after whom the celebrated Father De Smet mine was named—but who studiously kept his discovery a secret, fearing that, if known, it would demoralize the Indians. The old officer and the good father sat down together on the banks of the muddy Missouri, on a moonlight night, in 1870, and from some of the experiences of his thirty-five years of missionary life, he gave the following:

"I have heard a great many traditions among the Indians from their own mouths, speaking and understanding, as I do, many of their languages. Some of these traditions are very poetical, and suggestive of chapters in the Scriptures. The Indians all believe in spirits, good and evil, who again are subordinate to the one Great Spirit. When the young man becomes about sixteen years of age, he is placed under penance. That is, he is put by himself, generally in the woods, and is obliged to fast as long as his constitution can stand it. Some of these aspirants for future fame go without eating for seven or eight days. They do nothing during this time but sleep and dream. Toward the end, when they become feverish, they speak aloud in their dreams. The aged parents then listen, and if the young man, among his wandering words, mentions any particular plant, tree, bird, or animal, the name of such plant, tree, bird, or animal will be that of his particular spirit all through life. This name will be given to him after some appropriate adjectives have been added thereto. He will wear something suggestive of it about his person, and it is firmly believed by him that this special spirit will assist him in battle, and in hunting excursions, and that he will stand between him and danger.

"All the Indians believe, in their own crude way, of a future. Their idea of the hereafter is that when one of them dies he is piloted by his own individual spirit, toward an immense island, which, far off to the west, rises into a high mountain, reaching into the clouds, and upon the summit of which sits the Supreme Spirit. From this point of observation the Great Spirit overlooks the universe. Here He puts the sun to bed every night and sends out his moon and his stars, and hence he launches forth when angry his thunder and his lightning. On the island are the most beautiful rivers filled with fish, and the woods are alive with buffalo, and other desirable game. But it is not every departed brave who is permitted to enter this Garden of Eden. To reach the same the Indian has to cross a very wide and rapid stream by means of a dead tree lying across the same. In the middle of the stream and a few feet from the natural bridge, just beyond the reach of the wanderer, hangs a grape-vine, with clusters of ripe grapes. A good and brave Indian will cross the log without reaching for the grapes, for he is strong-hearted and needs no refreshments to help him along in his journey, but the faint-hearted, cowardly, lazy and bad Indian will go upon the log frightened and tired out; he will grasp for the grapes, fall into the torrent and be carried to a marshy place, where there are neither fish nor game, save a few coyotes and frogs.

"The origin of the human race some of them explain as follows: The Great Spirit first created a little boy who was upon the earth all alone for many years, but the boy felt lonesome, became melancholy and began crying until he fell asleep. The spirit then sent to him a little girl and she was called his sister and they lived as such together for many years. After the little girl grew up to be a woman she fell asleep one day and had a dream—that five men came to her hut and knocked for admittance, but that she took no notice of them, or opened the door to any of them except the last caller.

After awakening, the girl thought constantly of this dream, and, strange enough, in the course of time five men came to her cabin and asked her to go with them, but she refused all but the fifth and last one, who became her husband. They had at first but three children, one was called the Good Spirit and intercessor with the Great Spirit and the special friend of the Indian race; the second was called the Spirit of Fire and destruction and the great enemy of the white race; the third was called the White Rabbit, and ran away as soon as it was born. Upon the ascendancy of the white race, the first one fled, the second is now with them in their wars, and renders them brave; and the third occasionally appears and makes them fleet in their hunts. They are now awaiting the return of the first spirit. When he comes he will right the wrongs of his people and they will conquer all their enemies."

THE GAME OF BALL.

A THRILLING SCENE—TREACHERY OF THE INDIANS OUTWITTED.

NOTHING conduces so much to the pleasures of the Indians as an exciting game of ball, or a downright good dance. In these games their peculiar, excitable characteristics are fully developed, and both sexes indglge in the athletic sports. A game of ball is played in this way: A small place is prepared, and stakes are set for bounds, radiating from the center, when two parties are chosen, with leaders, who appear upon the field with bats or sticks about thirty-two inches long, to catch and throw the ball as the game progresses. "When one succeeds in getting the ball fairly in the pocket of his bat, he swings it aloft and throws it as far as he can toward the goal to which his party is working, taking care to send it, if possible, where some of his own side will take it up. Thus the ball is thrown and contended for till one party succeeds in casting it beyond the bounds of the opposite party. A hundred players on a side are sometimes engaged in this exciting game. Betting on the result often runs high. Moccasins, pipes, knives, hatchets, blankets, robes and guns are hung on the prize-pole. Not infrequently horses are staked on the issue, and sometimes even women. Old men and mothers are among the spectators, praising their swift-footed sons, and young wives and maidens are there to stimulate their husbands and lovers. This game is not confined to the warriors, but is also a favorite amusement of the Dakota maidens, who generally play for prizes offered by the chief, or warriors."

This reminds me of a most thrilling scene which occurred at a game of ball at Fort Mackenzie during the time when the French and English were contending for territory now belonging to the United States, and had it not been for the keen sagacity of the commander of the post, a most horrible massacre would have followed. It seems that the early French traders were favorites with the Indians, while the English were looked upon as interlopers, so that when war was declared between the two nations, the Indians sided with the French, and thus combining, made sad havoc with their enemy. Three forts had been established in the Indian country by the English, and two of these forts had been burned by the treacherous savages, and every soul killed. Flushed with the recent victory, the blood-thirsty Indians, with a large number of men, women and children, appeared in front of the third fort, and asked for an audience, as they desired peace. The commander, anxious to hear what the chiefs had to say, made his appearance on the ramparts and learned from the wily foe that they were tired of bloodshed; that they desired to bury the tomahawk and the scalping-knife, and to ever after live in harmony with the whites; so an arrangement was made to the effect, that on the morning of a beautiful day, stipulated by both parties, all the tribe should appear on the plateau below the fort, men, women and children, unarmed, and while the chiefs were negotiating a peace inside of the fort, the warriors outside were to engage in a game of ball. The conditions were explicit, that neither the soldiers, nor the Indians were to be armed, and this agreement was made as an earnest of good faith. The fort was located on a high rise of land, with a deep ditch encircling its base and a draw-bridge leading to it at a given point, over which parties must pass to get inside of the inclosure.

The plain below was level and beautiful, and the cannon of the fort frowned down upon it. The day for negotiations arrived, and with it came a large number of Indians with their squaws, headed by their chiefs; the bridge was swung; the soldiers appeared unarmed and listless, lying upon their guns; the Indians laughed and joked; the chiefs passed over the bridge, which was to be kept down as a passage-way to and from the fort, during the council meeting; the glittering eyes of the warriors glanced at the situation, as they entered the fortification, and then passed to the room of the commander, where they were met with the dignity which became their station. The room was a long one, on either side of which were blue curtains, and at the end of which, on an elevated seat, sat the commander. As is customary with the savages, they squat upon the floor, and after several had smoked the pipe of peace, commenced to discuss the terms upon which they had decided to agree. In the meantime the game of ball had been started. Hundreds of Indians were whooping and yelling and running now toward the fort, now from it; now clustering closer and closer to the draw-bridge, always preceded by the squaws, who drew their blankets closely about them ; now receding, now coming back again, like a great wave of the ocean ; while the soldiers gazed upon the scene and laughed at the grotesque figures moving about dotting the plain below. All the chiefs had smoked the pipe of peace in the council chamber but one. He halted; seemed anxious to gain a little more time and better terms, when the game of ball on the outside became more exciting; the Indians rushed toward the inclosure, when, with a terrible yell, which came from the tallest of the warriors in the crowd, and with terrific power, the ball was sent into the fort, and then, with another yell on the part of the rushing Indians, the squaws threw off their blankets, displaying weapons of war, which the Indians seized, and were soon clamoring over the draw-bridge, wild with a taste for blood.

In the meantime, when the last yell was given, the old chief in the council chamber, who had not yet smoked the pipe of peace, jumped to his feet and answered it; then the commander of the fort instantly gave a shrill whistle, and every gunner had his torch ready to discharge the cannon that pointed down upon the crowd below; every soldier was armed; every man was at his post; the blue curtains parted instantly, and two rows of guns confronted the treacherous chiefs! The old Indian, seeing that he was baffled, sent out another whoop, when the infuriated devils who were now crowding upon the bridge, suddenly fell back, and when still another yell came from the lips of the old chief, it was evident to the Indians on the outside, that their plan of massacre had been discovered! Not a muscle twitched in the face of the commandant; not a soldier stirred in his position; not a gunner moved who was commanded to dispute the passage of the bridge; when another whistle from the commander brought the men to a rest, and with it the bridge was drawn, the fort was saved, and the chiefs were prisoners, at the mercy of the whites! The commander paused for a moment, and then addressing his mortified foe, said: "You came to me with a lie upon your lips! You came to me with the belief that I would trust your lying tongues, so that, in a moment of confusion, you could dash upon my defenseless men and massacre them all in cold blood! But, thank God, your plans have failed, and I have only to give the word, and both you and your warriors and your women and your children, will be blotted from the face of the earth forever! See my big guns pointing down upon them? See twenty bullets aimed at your hearts! Mark my power! Treacherous, lying, deceitful dogs! the paleface has met you with your own weapons; shall he deal out to you that which you intended to deal out to him? No; if the paleface is brave, he is also magnanimous! If the paleface has beaten you by precautionary measures, he is also generous! If the paleface has you and your people in his power, he can afford to be great, grand and merciful!"

Then rising and waving his hand, he said to his astonished enemies: "Go!" A universal "ho! ho!" (yes, yes; bravo!) followed the remark of the officer, when the Indians arose and, marching boldly to the commander, the head chief said:

"You have saved the lives of our people! You have saved our own lives! You have taught us how to live! You have shown us that the heart of the paleface is good—that the heart of the Indian is bad. We come no longer to you with two tongues. We come to you in the presence of the Great Spirit, whom we wish to bear testimony to the fact, that from this day, and forever after, we shall always be the friends of the whites, who have not only convinced us that they are brave and merciful, but that they are wise and magnanimous. We lay our lives at your feet. Nis-is-shin ne-car-nis i-to—(Good best friends forever)!"

"Go!" again uttered the commander. "Tell your people the paleface desires only peace, truth, manhood, justice, right, and if they will come to him with one tongue, and be governed by the principles here enunciated, that then we can bury the tomahawk and the scalping-knife, and live kindly together as one people. Go!"

The chiefs moved out into the open space of the fort with a bold step, and passed down on to the drawbridge, and across it to the plateau below, where they were received with great joy by the baffled warriors, who supposed that their head men had been put to death; and when it became known how magnanimously they had been treated by the commandant, they burst into a wild, weird shriek, that went booming through the fort and died in echoes among the hills.

The sun went down that night on many happy hearts within the fortification and on a happy tribe of Indians who had resolved to lead a different and a better life, which resolution was faithfully kept for many years afterward.

Then there was another game of ball on the same plateau below the fort; another scene of mirth; another contest for victory; and among the participants were the soldiers and the warriors, the commander and the chiefs; and then hands of friendship were grasped; and words of kindness were spoken and farewells were uttered, and the fort was vacated and the soldiers departed, and the red men of the forest gathered in sadness about their tepee fires and recounted over again the memorable scenes of a most remarkable event—THAT GAME OF BALL.

PA-HA-WA-KAN.

THE SACRED DESCENT, OR ONK-TO-MEE—BAD SPIRIT NE-BE-NAU-BAIG—WATER SPIRIT, OR DEVIL'S LAKE.

THIS is not a Sioux legend, but was told to Tacangi by a Blackfoot woman, who had been long a prisoner among the Sioux. Formerly all that country lying between the Missouri river on the east, and the Rocky mountains on the west, is said to have been a garden of paradise overflowing with game, etc., but as this legend runs, was changed in three days to what it now is. The point designated is no doubt what is at present known as the Bad Lands, including the buttes which appear in that country, and the legend has more in it than the casual observer would at first suspect. The Blackfoot squaw says:

"An Indian band, camped upon the banks of the Missouri, had sent to a few of their brethren who were located at the foot of a very large mound, some distance from them, to say that for three days the Prophet, or Medicine Man of their band had been in a swoon, and that they had watched him during that time and his lips had never ceased to move as in prayer, and begged them to join them in offerings to the Great Spirit, as they feared some calamity was about to befall them. The mound Indians were a desperate class—a band mostly murderers, and knowing their own wickedness, this information made them feel sad. Calling all his braves together, the chief told them the news—

what he had heard from the other Indians—and besought them to go each one at once and make offerings. All did so, and donning gay garments, went into mourning. That same night, at 12 o'clock, the few who slept were awakened by terrific peals of thunder, the rain falling like knives upon their tepees, the lightning darting apparently into their very lodges, and a wind blew that threatened every moment to tear their homes to pieces.

"All at once there was a great noise as of crying in the camp. Amid confusion and bustle, all ran out to see what it was, when, suddenly, as it were, the whole heavens gave way, and fell upon the top of the mound, while the Indians threw themselves upon the ground, not daring to look up. Again the heavens seemed to fall and close upon the mound, and this time accompanied with great darkness. Then a sudden panic seized upon them all, and with one accord, they rushed into their wigwam. What happened furthermore no one knew, as they recollect, until morning, when awakened as it were from sleep, although they had not slept, that a strange sight met their view! The mountains were black as if scorched by lightning; whole country deadened, and smoke issuing from the top of some of the mounds. One night had rendered the county a desert. They looked for their horses—all were dead! Then in camp loud mourning sounds came from the women; their meats and provisions were all full of worms! They knew then they must now starve unless they moved on, and amid universal lamentations, they took up their trail and marched south. Everywhere the country was the same. At night some of their mounds spit out fire, and will-o'-the-wisps floated around everywhere, trying to lure them to destruction. The earth rumbled and the air was thick with sulphur.

"For three days they traveled thus, when all of a sudden they came to a large body of water, where formerly they had roamed amid a luxuriant sea of tropical plants, and where birds of gay plumage sang their morning songs. All was now dark, gloomy, and dead. Gone were the forest songsters and the young gazelle with its dove eyes; gone the flowers; gone the game; gone the grand trees, and the gentle summer breeze; and in their places were a vast sheet of water, with upheavals of rock, and black, smoldering ruins, and dark clouds, and curling smoke, and gloomy figures, dancing in the distance. They changed their course, and, winding around the lake, came to a mound which hid the water from their view, and here they heard what appeared to them to be human voices. They listened, and the song was so wild and so weird that they could not stir—they were spell-bound.

'Changing, swinging, singing, ringing,
Dancing Devils all are we;
Piping, peeping, peering, creeping,
How we mingle in our glee.
Ho! ho! shovel them in!
Shovel them in!
'Tis the reward of early sin!

'Now we laugh and now we grin,
He! he! and ho! ho!
Pitch them up and pitch them in,
He! he! and ho! ho!
Along the slimy banks we go,
With our he! he! and ho! ho!'

"Several of the Indians stealthily crept to the top of the mound and peering over beheld a scene of the most startling character. On the shore but a short distance from them was a very large animal, apparently resembling the human race—with enormous, protruding ears, peculiar hoofs, a dark swarthy face, horribly distorted; a gay fiery sash about his loins, a long caudal extremity resting upon the ground, and in his hands a wooden pitchfork, which he used with great dexterity. Gathered about him were no less than a thousand young figures resembling the older one, and when they sang they all swayed to and fro, pitching into the lake what appeared to be human bodies. At the end of each verse of the song the earth rumbled with a loud noise, fire belched out from the many small mounds surrounding the lake; dark, pitchy smoke filled the atmosphere and all the region round about was dense with the smell of sulphur; and at this point the song became demoniacal, and the dancing figures opened up to the imagination a vivid picture of hell itself, especially as they swayed back and forth and sang 'He! he! and ho! ho!' Confused, frightened, horrified at what they had seen, the Indians ran down the mound, over the blackened earth, screaming as they ran 'Oonk-to-mee, Ne-be-nau-baig!' Devil's lake! Devil's lake, and from that day to this the lake has ever borne this peculiar name. They continued rapidly on their march south for three days, when the country appeared to grow better; and, finally, when they approached a game section, they all stopped, offered sacrifices, and then only did the earth cease to rumble and the air begin to be pure. But the Indians never after could remain in that country.

"Thus, for the sins of a small portion of a nation, was a whole people made to suffer, and a country, which before was a paradise, became a desert."

This legend contains more truth than fiction, for I have traveled all over this land and have marked its peculiar characteristics. After leaving Bismarck, on the one side, and Cheyenne and Sidney on the other, great plains stretch out before the eye, broken only by immense masses of rock, which are lifted high up in the air, and then the vision is again uninterrupted for miles and miles. How these huge piles of stones came upon these vast plains, isolated, as it were, without a cause, is accounted for only on the ground, that at some period in the past, a great volcanic eruption took place in the northeast, and passing along southwest, broke through the thinnest crust of the earth, and left these heavy deposits of rock. In corroboration of this theory, I note the fact that all these buttes come along in a straight line from the northeast to the southwest; that is, here would be a large uplift, some three or four hundred feet high, while several miles southwest, would be another, and so on, for miles and miles, across these great plains. These uplifts, at a distance, present the appearance of houses and barns, but as you approach them, the illusion disappears.

Then, again, we find mounds, beneath which is rock, the volcanic force not having been strong enough to throw the stone to the surface. Following these buttes to the Missouri river on the east side, we discover where the volcanic fires have spent their fury on the edge of the river, great peaks or mountains appearing, upon the tops of which I found black, scarified rocks, mixed with sulphur, mica and iron slag, very clearly indicating that the volcanic wave from the northeast was arrested in its progress by the river, and hence left its mark. No doubt, at the time this eruption took place, the sun was darkened, the earth shook and rumbled, and the air was full of sulphur and falling stones, and it was probably at or about this period that this legend originated, based upon a fact instead of fiction. So, too, I may say of the previous beauty of the country and its surroundings; its animals, its foliage, its game. The remains of some of the largest turtles ever known have been found in this region; also of defunct wild beasts, of gigantic size; trunks of great trees have been discovered in the bowels of the earth. Petrified wood is obtained here in great abundance; the soil is very rich —a vegetable mold—all going to show, that at one period in the history of this country it was a paradise—the loved home of the Indian, or the mound-builders—but that suddenly its beauty was destroyed; its animals killed; its contour changed; its pure water turned to alkali; its flowers and shrubbery obliterated; not by an act of the Great Spirit, as is believed by the Indians, but by a law of nature, producing just exactly what the exterior surface of the earth demonstrates, has been produced by NATURAL CAUSES. No one who has traveled that country and knows anything of its history, can arrive at any other conclusion; so that this legend is especially interesting as opening up a new train of thought of vast importance for further researches in the Great Northwest.

OLD BETS.

AZA-YA-MAN-KA-WAN; OR BERRY PICKER.

THE familiar face of Old Bets, an Indian squaw, peered in upon my vision for about twenty years, when, all of a sudden, it disappeared, and the news came that she was dead! Very few who met her wrinkled face, her laughing eyes, her grotesque figure, or heard her whining voice asking for "kosh-poppy," or money, knew of the romantic history attached to that old squaw, as she almost daily paraded the streets of a frontier city and sold her moccasins or begged for aid. The weight of years, the burden of trouble, silent grief, patient forebearance, all leave their impress behind, and the Indian is not exempt from the general law. Who knows, or can divine the history of that old man, tottering under the load of a life of suffering? Who could realize that in his early days he stole the hearts of women, electrified men, and moved the masses with his eloquence? Now, how useless! Who could imagine even, the early triumphs, the bewitching beauty, the imcomparable charms of that young girl, who, threading life's thoroughfare, drew after her hundreds of admirers? Now, that bent-over, gray-haired, bowed-down form! how changed! So each and every one has a history and must, in turn, pass out of youth and vigor, and beauty, and manhood, and womanhood, into the silent, stealthy tread of old age, groping down the valley of death, hoping to catch a glimpse on the other shore of that light which burns forever!

Old Bets was once young and handsome, and she drew after her many lovers. Born at the confluence of two rivers—the Mississippi and the Minnesota—her childhood was passed among the scenes of her final death; but her early girlhood was out among the wild scenery of her tribe, where danger confronted the red men of the plains, and acts of valor crowned the warrior with undying fame! Young Bets was greatly loved, not only for her beauty, but for her kind disposition, as well as for her bravery; so it came to pass that a young man who had won great renown in the tribe, sought the hand of the young girl in marriage, and in turn she looked upon his attention, with favor. Her brother, however, being himself a warrior and a medicine man, objected to the match upon the ground that his sister's suitor had, in the past, wronged him, and he should never darken the door of his tepee, even if he did—as he was willing to—make amends for the injury given.

The merry laugh of the maiden gradually died away. Her joyous nature turned to soberness, as she thought of the young heart which beat only for her, and, in turn, before she was aware of it, her tenderest feelings were wrapped up in the welfare of the young and ardent lover, whose image had become a part of her own existence. She besought her brother to forgive the young warrior. She assured him her happiness depended upon her union with him, but the stoical face and the hardened heart would not relax, and she turned away with great sorrow and entered the forest near by, where, unexpectedly she met Chig-go-nia, her best and dearest friend.

Here the interview terminated with a solemn resolve

to die for each other, and on the morrow the two were to quietly meet, bid good-bye to the old associations, and mounted on ponies, pass away west as man and wife.

With the rising of the sun the young and lovely Berry Picker had fled, and with her Chig-go-nia. Her brother whose name was He-in-da-koo, was soon aware of what had occurred, and mounted on one of his fleetest ponies, and well armed, he started in pursuit. About noon he overtook the flying couple, who, conscious of his desperate hatred and unrelenting ferocity, redoubled their speed; the warrior, however, gained upon them until their horses were all soon neck and neck, and speeding rapidly over the plain together. Young Bets' brother then rode in front, and drawing his horses head across the path of the lover, sought to cut him down with his tomahawk. His sister pleaded for his life, but seeing that her pleadings were all in vain, she reigned in her pony, brought him close to the side of her lover, and with one spring from her animal landed in his lap. With one arm about the waist of his love, the young man fought bravely for his life, but encumbered with the maiden, he fought to great disadvantage; when, all of a sudden, his antagonist struck him with his tomahawk on the head from behind, and the young man sank to the earth, and in the arms of his sweetheart breathed out his last farewell. The maiden was carried back into camp, and though she subsequently married a man of note in her tribe, yet the great sorrow of her early love never left her, and traces of that sorrow could be seen upon her face, even in her old age.

Old Bets was born at a place called Mendota, and

died a few years ago at the age of seventy-five years, although, from her weather-beaten and care-worn appearance, many supposed her to be over one hundred years. She married Iron Sword, and had several children, one of whom, Ta-opi, became converted to Christianity and aided very considerably toward elevating and civilizing his tribe.

For many years this inoffensive old woman traveled the streets of the white man's city, and became a a marked character both to the citizens and to strangers. I remember her as the possessor of a wrinkled face, peculiar eyes, disheveled hair, large mouth, uncovered neck, uncouth form, but always with her cheerful "ho-hos," as she plodded along under the weight of years, and of her great, unknown sorrow. She was a kind and devoted friend of the whites; was the means of saving several lives during the massacre in Minnesota, in 1861, and before her death became quite poor, but it is a credit to humanity to be able to state, that she was aided by pecuniary help during her sickness, and finally died in the Christian belief, and was accorded a Christian burial. The portrait of her, which we present, is an excellent one, and was taken only a short time before her death. Good-bye, OLD BETS.

WA-ZI-YA* AND THE ENCHANTED KNIFE.

ONCE upon a time there was an old woman, who had an only son, and what is remarkable, he was born with a handkerchief about his neck, and was considered by the Indians, a great prodigy. The child grew to be a general favorite with everybody, and at three years of age, could hunt and fish as well as any Indian. When about thirteen years of age, the camp broke up and moved down the river to trade with an old medicine man who kept roots, etc., for sale, and also to lay in their medicines for the hunting season. The old woman was sick at the time, and consequently she and her little boy were the only ones left on the old camp ground. It was during this solitude and time for thought, which sickness offers, that the tales of the wild and rapacious Wa-zi-ya floated across her memory; and there was scarcely an evening that she did not take occasion to warn her boy about going in a northerly direction in his rambles. "My son," she would say, "thou art the only prop of my old age. If I lose thee I may well mourn. Whilst rearing thee I have always endeavored to instruct thee, and now, as thou art big enough, warn thee against those cruel demons who inhabit the North. The Wa-zi-ya is ever a foe to the homes of our people, and should one suddenly meet thee, death would be your reward."

* The god of the North, or Winter, a fabled spirit who dwells in the frozen North in a great tepee of ice and snow. From his mouth and nostrils he blows the cold blast of winter.

The youth hung his head in silence; he could not realize the existence of such cruel monsters as his mother had depicted, and it awakened in him a curiosity to know more of them. "Well," thought he, "if Wa-zi-ya be such a foe to mankind, why don't they kill him? Is he too big for them to kill?" And he half wished that he could see one, just to know what kind of beings they were. It is thus that curiosity draws us on to our own destruction. The more he thought of it, the more intense became his desire to see one, and by degrees this thoughtless curiosity grew so upon him that he would wander for miles toward the north, then suddenly become alarmed and return. The subject so preyed upon his mind that he made a resolution to go and see for himself. Accordingly, one evening, after his mother had recovered from her sickness, he took his bows and arrows and started out, determined not to come back until he had seen and learned more of the dreadful Wa-zi-ya. Thoughtfulness never fails of its punishment. Throughout the whole day he traveled, never dreaming of eating—in fact forgetting that he had no food whatever with him, until night fell upon him, and he lay down with his blanket around him and was soon fast asleep. In the morning early he awakened, and, as usual, his first thought was of Wa-zi-ya; but it was only for a few moments that his mind ran in that direction, for hunger soon made him conscious of its terrible pang. It was only then that he began to realize his situation. A long day's travel from home, with no food in his bundle, and to all appearances, no game of any kind around him—in a moment these thoughts impressed themselves upon him, and then, throwing himself upon the ground, he burst into tears. Unbinding the handkerchief from his neck—the same he was born with—he attempted to put it to his eyes, but a blast of wind carried it out of his hand, and it alighted some distance from him. He runs to get it! Great Spirit!—it lies spread out, and upon it food of all kinds. Drying his eyes he eats, then rises and pursues his journey.

Toward noon he sees what appears to be a fort and he approaches it, finding it to be an immense building, and to his wondering eyes the home of Wa-zi-ya. Looking in at the open door he sees no one; he enters and a horrible sight meets his view! Around the room were the heads of those slain; skulls nailed to the wall and under each head was fastened a hand severed at the wrist. His blood ran cold, and while meditating what he should do, he heard a noise like thunder, and in comes Wa-zi-ya. "I smell something," said the great monster! The boy hides behind a post, but Wa-zi-ya smells him out and takes him in his hand. "Naw-a-pesk-ta, se-ce-ca!" "I will eat you up!" Boy regains courage; begs him not to eat him. "Hungry!—must," said the monster. Boy says: "I will give you plenty to eat." The great giant laughs and says—"Wi-ca-ka-wo!" You can't do it. But the boy spreads his handkerchief upon the ground and immediately it is covered with food. Wa-zi-ya fills himself, and then turning to the little stranger, says: "Ha! my boy, this will do; now you may go home unharmed." Boy starts to go, but is called back. Wa-zi-ya wants the handkerchief, but the boy is unwilling to part with it. The giant says he must have it; he will give him a flute for it.

"What can I do with the flute?" asked the boy.

Call an army of genii when in need. The boy will not consent; goes home; does not tell his mother, but at the first favorable opportunity, goes again. Wa-zi-ya asks him for more food, for he has come to like the boy, but the boy pretends not to hear him. The giant asks again, and says: "If you will produce a supper as good as the last, I will give you this," showing him a knife. "And what good will this do me?" asks the boy. "Oh, it does whatever its possessor tells it to." Boy consents and receives the knife. Wa-zi-ya immediately falls to eating the provisions, and while thus engaged the boy walks off a short distance, takes out knife, tells it to cut Wa-zi-ya's head off, and off it comes! Boy runs home, tells his mother, and then there is great rejoicing, and amid it all orange trees spring up and bear oranges; figs grow in great abundance; flowers bloom; birds sing; all sorts of game cluster in the bushes; fishes sport in the rivers and in the lakes; buffalo surround the camp; the air is mild and balmy; the Indians gather in immense numbers, and there is a great feast, for the boy, born with a handkerchief about his neck, has killed the god of the North, or Winter; has broken down his great temple of ice and snow; has turned his cold and cheerless blasts into perennial summer; has brought joy and happiness and plenty to the Dakota nation.

OPINIONS, BELIEFS AND CUSTOMS OF THE INDIANS.

WE all have supposed that the Indians draw directly from nature their beliefs, their opinions and their customs, as we have no knowledge that a people existed on the American Continent, anterior to them, except the vague conception of a pre-historic race, about which we know but very little; hence, whatever their customs and beliefs may be, they are original with themselves. And yet we can trace their peculiar characteristics to the Arabs, and many of their religious ceremonies to the Jews, leaving one to infer that at a remote period in the past, the so-called American Indian, or rather his descendants, were inhabitants of the Old World, and transplanted to the new, many customs and beliefs supposed to belong solely to themselves, but which have a greater antiquity than the American continent itself. Donnelly in his "Atlantis," recently published, advances some cogent reasons and authorities, to prove, that at one time the two oceans were connected by land, and that on an island called "Atlantis," then existing in the ocean, there lived a race of people much more intelligent than the American Indian, and from whom the Indians sprung; or, if he did not originate there, he came into the western hemisphere over this land, and brought with him some of the beliefs and traditions of the Old World. Donnelly claims that Atlantis was sunk in the ocean, and totally destroyed.

When among the Bois Fortes Indians years ago, my camp was visited by two sons of the chiefs, accompanied by their squaws or wives, and after the usual salutation—"Booshu Nechee," how to do, friend (the Indian never says good-morning or good-evening, but it is either friend or foe), we set before them a good, solid dinner of bread, coffee, pork and beans, and of which they partook plentifully. One of the women had in her arms a bundle, and I observed that every time she eat, she passed a piece of bread or a few beans to the mysterious something she cuddled to her bosom so affectionately. After she had left, I said to my interpreter—"What did that squaw have in her arms?" to which he quickly replied—"Why the bones or skeleton of a baby!" "Is that their habit?" I inquired. "Oh, yes," he replied. "When a child dies, through a process known to these Indians, the body is preserved until the flesh is all gone, and the skin is drawn tightly over the bones; then the remains are decorated in its little garments, embroidered with beads, its wee playthings are sewed up among the clothing and the mother is obliged to carry the child wherever she goes—or rather the skeleton—until another baby is born or the father dies, when it is put away. At every meal the mother feeds the inanimate remains, believing that this is necessary to sustain its existence on its way to the spirit world, and hence what you have seen, is only a religious duty of a parent to its offspring."

Indian adults are buried with their wands of red, white and blue, to be used soon after death to keep off the bad and tempting spirits, when they reach the shores of the happy hunting ground (see legend of Min-ne-too-ka); so also are they buried with their guns, their blankets, etc.; and if a warrior of note dies, his ponies are killed at his grave, so that he may have horses to ride in the other world. Food is also left at their tombs for their sustenance. Their belief in the future is very strong, as these incidents would indicate.

A feeling exists between a mother and her children, by which, no matter how far apart they may be, she can tell when they are suffering or in danger. There are not a few Sioux women who do not in some measure believe in this, and many are the tales that are told of the exercise of this strange power. There are also many white women who believe in this influence, for they have had considerable experience in this direction. The Indians formerly elevated their dead upon poles or scaffolds, where they remained for one year; now they bury them in the ground, and they are always disposed of with their heads to one of the four cardinal points of the compass. Many inter them with their heads to the north and feet to the south, since they believe that the spirit of the Indians will travel south to the land of ease and comfort; yet, many imagine that their spirits will go west; others think that the east is the final abode of mortality, made immortal by some invisible power. The idea that everything on the earth is acted upon by spirits pervades all the action of the Dakotas. They believe that the "wangi's" spirit—though the same word means skeleton—inhabits the ravines and hollows, and for that season they bury their dead usually upon the edge of some coolie or ravine, that the spirit may return to the body at pleasure. They also believe that good and evil spirits walk the earth and influence their actions.

The divinities of the Sioux are legion. The air, the

earth, the water, the heavens, and even fire itself, all have their separate divinities and spirits of evil. Everything is linked with darkness and terror, except the one great, the incomprehensible, the silent God. Deities whose sole object is evil, are ever around them, and a sudden death calls them up in all their terror, working upon the minds of a few, and bringing fear to children and to old women. The Wa-kan-tan-ka, or Great Spirit of the Sioux, is the same being as the god of the Saxon, the Goda of the Persian, the Khoda of the Sanscrit, and the Koda of the Sioux. Did these deities originate among themselves? They agree in attributes with the divinities of foreign mythologies, but how did the Indians know of these mythologies if they were the first and only original inhabitants on the American continent? Whence came their idea of deities and mythology, except that they originated in the long past, and have been handed down from a remote age to the present? I am forced to believe that such is the fact, and that the Indian is the descendant of a race of people who formerly lived in Europe, but which is now extinct.

THE LAST MAN!—STRANGE BELIEFS.

THE Mandan Indians, many years ago, had a very clear conception of the flood, and celebrated the event in quite an interesting manner. Many of these Indians were really white—it seems a paradoxium to call them Indians—with hazel, gray and blue eyes, for, no doubt, they were the descendants of a white race.

Catlin, in a recent work, says: "On the day set apart for the commencement of the ceremonies in commemoration of the flood, a solitary figure is seen approaching the village. During the deafening din and confusion within the pickets of the village, the figure discovered on the prairie, continued to approach with a dignified step, and in a right line toward the village; all eyes were upon him, and he at length made his appearance within the pickets and proceeded toward the center of the village where all the chiefs and braves stood ready to receive him, which they did in a cordial manner, by shaking hands, recognizing him as an old acquaintance and pronouncing his name, Nu-mohk-muck-a-nah, the first, or only man. The body of this strange personage, which was chiefly naked, was painted with white clay, so as to resemble, at a distance, a white man. He enters the medicine lodge and goes through certain mysterious ceremonies. During the whole of this day, Nu-mohk-muck-a-nah, traveled through the village, stopping in front of each man's tepee, and crying until the owner of the lodge came out and asked who he was and what was the matter? To which he replied by narrating the sad catastrophe which had happened on the earth's surface by the overflowing of the waters, saying that he was the only person saved from the universal calamity; that he landed his big canoe on a high mountain in the west, where he now resides; that he has come to open the medicine lodge, which must needs receive a present of an edged tool from the owner of every wigwam, that it may be sacrificed to the water; for, he says, if this is not done there will be another flood and no one will be saved, as it was with such tools that the big canoe was made.

"Having visited every lodge in the village during the day, and having received such a present from each as a hatchet, a knife, etc., he places them in the medicine lodge; and on the last day of the ceremony they are thrown into a deep place in the river—sacrificed to the spirit of the waters."

The Dakotas have a similar belief, clearly showing that the aborigines or this country must have had, at least, traditionary information of the Old World.

The Dakotas believe that the earth is an extended plain. This belief, alone, is evidence of nothing, for all rude nations have formed exactly such an idea of it, but when the Dakota adds to this his belief that the further north you go, the higher the ground becomes, until it terminates in lofty mountains, behind which the sun is hid in the night as he travels east to resume his diurnal course to the west again, it is easy enough to recognize in this the general belief of ancient India, that "the sun revolves around a lofty northern mountain, producing day when on one side and night when on the other."

To have the hair cut short, is esteemed by all Indians

a great disgrace. The Dakotas especially deem it so, since it was a part of the punishment of a murderer, and was also the reward of treachery. A Dakota woman, however, and sometimes a young brave, will vow to cut off her or his hair in case an earnestly wished-for event transpires happily; but even under such circumstances they do not cut it off short, but merely clip a few hairs. An Indian's face painted black, indicates his desire to kill somebody. (See article, "A Run for Life.")

Praying or invoking and vowing are quite common among the Sioux. A brave starts upon a war-party and is suddenly surrounded by the enemy with but little hope of escape. Making a vow to Ta-kux-kanx-kan, or some other divinity that he will make a certain number of beasts in his honor, or that he will go upon so many war-parties during the ensuing year, if the God will only assist him, or some other vow, he plunges into the fight. If he escapes he is sure to keep his vow, for it is a thing sacred, in his mind, and not to be trifled with. An Indian hunting in the woods loses his way, becomes frightened and thinks he is in great danger. He immediately makes a vow, that if he is saved, he will assume this or that character for such a length of time; and on reaching home in safety he at once does so. In fact the Mohammedan pilgrims or the Hindoo faquirs are not more earnest in their vows nor more scrupulous in performing them than are the Dakotas. They are superstitious in the extreme, and look upon a broken vow as irreparable and certain to call down the anger of the spirits upon them. It was this superstitious feeling which found vent when they heard for the first time, the report of a rifle, upon which they cried out: "Wa-kan-c," this is supernatural; and the same spirit was evinced when they first saw the mariner's compass. The chief would frequently call for a sight of it, and tell his braves that the white men were spirits, capable of doing everything. They believe in the existence of numbers of Wan-a-gi-dan, or spirits, whose sole business is to plague and torment poor humanity. They do not believe that these spirits are able to cause death, but give to them nearly the same attributes that we do to our elf-sprites or fairies.

Previous to the time when they obtained horses—scarcely a century ago—the lot of the Dakota woman was hard indeed. Upon a journey they were forced to pack all the household stuff, including their tents, upon their backs; and though they used the large wolf-dog for packing, by placing transverse poles across his back, fastened together over the shoulders—the other ends trailing upon the ground—yet the main packing had to be done upon their own shoulders. Before starting in the morning, the men usually point out the place at which they are to camp for the night; and for that point the squaws and children, each with their packs upon their backs, start at once, while the men make a detour over the prairie through the woods, in search of game. My own horse was the first animal of the kind the Indians on Vermilion lake, in the northern portion of Minnesota and near the Canadian line, had ever seen and when he appeared in full view, they became greatly excited and frightened; ran, screamed and hid, as they thought it was a Great Spirit. This was in the year 1865.

Among the Yankton Indians, the first who obtained a gun, endeavored to make it go off, as he supposed the white man of whom he bought it made it go—*without loading*—and after repeated failures, he became enraged, and broke it over the head of his wife. Another Indian, having been taught how to load it, put in too much powder, with a foot of wadding, and he was very much surprised to find himself upon his back, after the discharge, and thinking one near him had struck him, he pitched into the crowd promiscuously and got beautifully thrashed!

The young Indian women have a peculiar kind of broth which they give the men to make them fall desperately in love with them. Various tricks are devised to conceal the nature of this medicine, and to induce the warrior to drink it. When mixed with "Scoot-a-wa-boo," or fire-water, it is irresistible, as all whisky toddies are.

An Indian who had been wounded and was about to die, requested that his horse might be gaily caparisoned and brought to his hospital window, so that he might touch the animal. He then took from his medicine bag a large cake of maple sugar, and held it forth. It may seem strange, but it is true, that the beast ate it from his hand. The invalid's features were radiant with delight as he fell back upon the pillow exhausted. His horse had eaten of the sugar, he said, and he was now sure of a favorable reception and comfortable quarters in the other world. Half an hour later he breathed his last.

Jonathan Carver, one of the early explorers, says:

"One formality among the Nan-dow-essies in mourning for the dead, is very different from any mode I observed in the other nations through which I passed. The men, to show how great their sorrow is, pierce the flesh of their arms above the elbows with arrows, and the women cut and gash their legs with broken flints until the blood flows plentifully.

"After the breath is departed, the body is dressed in the same attire it usually wore; the face of the deceased is painted, and he is seated in an erect posture on a mat or skin, placed in the middle of the hut, with his weapons by his side. His relatives seated around him, each in turn harangue the deceased; and, if he has been a great warrior, recount his heroic actions nearly to the following purport, which, in the Indian language, is extremely poetical and pleasing:

"'You still sit among us, brother; your person retains its usual resemblance and continues similar to ours, without any visible deficiency, except it has lost the power of action. But, whither is that breath flown, which, a few hours ago sent up smoke to the Great Spirit? Why are those lips silent, that lately delivered to us expressions and pleasing language? Why are those feet motionless that a few hours ago were fleeter than the deer on yonder mountains? Why useless hang those arms that could climb the tallest tree or draw the toughest bow? Alas, every part of that frame, which we beheld with admiration and wonder, has now become as inanimate as it was three hundred years ago! We will not, hower, bemoan thee as if thou wast forever lost to us, or that thy name would be buried in oblivion; thy soul yet lives in the great country of spirits, with those of thy nation that have gone before thee; and though we are left behind to perpetuate thy fame, we will one day join thee.

"'Actuated by the respect we bore thee whilst living, we now come to tender thee the last act of kindness in our power; that thy body might not be neglected on the plains and become a prey to the beasts of the fields or fowls of the air, we will take care to lay it with those of thy predecessors that have gone before thee, hoping at the same time that thy spirit will feed their spirits, and be ready to receive ours when we shall also arrive at the great country of souls.'" Toon-hay-hay means "woe is me," a lament for the dead.

In the "Desert of the Exodus," by Palmer, I find a similar ceremony over the death of a member of one of the Arab tribes, which leads me to conclude that the Indians obtained this ceremony from the Arabs, or it originally came from the Old World. The writer says:

"When a Bedouin dies the corpse is at once taken out of the tent to a convenient place, washed with soap and water and shrouded. A bag containing a little corn is placed beside it, and it is immediately buried. As soon as it is placed in the grave the friends of the deceased beat upon the ground with a stick, recite the Fatihah and cry out: 'Oh, thou most compassionate! have mercy upon us, gracious God!' Then they tap with a small pick-ax at the head of the grave and address the deceased in these words: 'When the twain Green Angels shall question and examine thee, say: 'The feaster makes merry, the wolf prowls, and man's lot is still the same, but I have done with all these things. The side tree is thy aunt and the palm tree thy mother.' Each one then throws a little dirt into the grave, exclaiming as he does so: 'God have mercy upon thee,' and the party adjourns to a feast in the tent of the deceased. Another entertainment is given in honor of his memory after the lapse of four months. When a death occurs in an encampment the women of the family at once go outside of the tent, and taking off their head dresses, commence a loud and impassioned wailing, which they continue throughout the day."

The Indians call a steamboat "the house that walks on the waters," and a humming bird they declare comes from the land of the rainbow.

Each feather worn by a warrior represents an enemy slain or captured—man, woman or child. Feathers among the Dakotas have very different significations according to the way in which they are painted or notched. The only feathers that have any meaning attached to them, are those of the eagle. Each feather stands for an enemy killed, but very frequently one feather only is used to designate the number slain. Then an eagle feather with a round dot of red paint upon it, the size of a bullet, denotes that the wearer has slain an enemy by shooting with a bullet, and as many dots of this kind as there are upon the feather, so many enemies have been slain.

The Chippewas tell this story: The various birds met together one day to try which could fly the highest. Some flew up very swift, but soon got tired and were passed by others of stronger wing. But the eagle went up beyond them all, and was ready to claim the victory, when, the gray linnet, a very small bird, flew from the eagle's back, where it had perched unperceived, and, being fresh and unexhausted, succeeded in going the highest. When the birds came down and met in council to award the prize, it was given to the eagle, because that bird had not only gone up nearer to the sun than any of the larger birds, but it had carried the linnet on its back. For this reason the eagle's feathers became the most honorable marks of distinction a warrior could wear.

Indians not only pick out all the hair from their faces, but from their bodies. I have seen Indians, however, with good beards, but they are rare. It is a peculiar feature in the history of the race, that they totally abhor hair, except upon the head, and this custom of pulling it out, has a deeper significance than appears upon the surface. Did the savages originate from a people who once wore beards, and did some great event prejudice them against hair, or, are they a distinct race, descendants only from themselves?

It is worthy of remark, that a chief, in speech, always calls the country owned by his nation—"Ma-ko-ee Mi-ta-wa"—my country; while the braves usually say, "Ma-ko-ee un-kit-a-wa-pi,"—our country, a distinction which some have imagined is a relic of the old regal claim to all the national domain, as it was among the ancient Hindoo and other eastern nations.

The Indians have many feasts. Indeed, fighting, feasting and dancing are the prominent elements of their nature. The Virgin feast, however, is a sacred right and has much to commend it. None but Virgins are permitted to engage in the ceremony, and it is intended to compliment, retain and perpetuate the chastity of Indian maidens. Only unpolluted girls are permitted to touch the sacred armor of the Dakota warriors, and during the ceremony, they use white cedar, which is considered wa-kan, or sacred. Mrs. Eastman says that the "Sacred Ring" around the feast of the Virgins, is formed by armed warriors sitting, and none but a Virgin must enter this ring. The warrior who knows, is bound on honor and by old sacred custom, to expose and publicly denounce any tarnished maiden who dares to enter this ring, and his word cannot be questioned—even by the chiefs.

The mode of courtship among the sexes differs somewhat with the various tribes of Indians of the Northwest, but the ultimate end of obtaining a wife—by purchase—is almost universal. Among some of the tribes of the Chippewas, the courtship is usually in this way: The loving girl, if she favors a young man, removes from the side of her mother in the tepee, where she usually sleeps, and cuddles up in her blanket on the left of the entrance to the wigwam. The young man goes round the tepee three times, and if she does not move during these trips, he is assured that his overtures are acceptable. He goes home, and at the expiration of three nights comes again, and finding his girl still in the place where he left her, he slips in under the blanket, where the courtship is carried on during the greater portion of the night. Then, if everything is agreeable, he formally asks the father for the hand of his daughter, and proffers certain articles of value, a horse, or canoe, or blanket, and when the trade is completed, the two are married.

Some tribes on the Missouri river insist that the man who wants his girl, must catch her while on horseback, and for this purpose a very fleet pony is obtained, the girl placed upon it, and the contending lovers are obliged to follow, and the one who catches the flying maiden first, can claim her as his wife, whether she loves him or not. Of course woman's wits usually win, for, knowing who they want, they guide their horses so as to fall into the hands of their lovers, irrespective of the speed of the various animals.

There is a striking resemblance between the mode of courtship and marriage of a tribe of Arabs, called the Bedouin, and the North American Indians. Palmer, in his work, says:

"The intending bridegroom, with five or six friends, call upon the father of the girl, who prepares and sets before them a bowl of food and some coffee, and when they have partaken of the refreshments, the bridegroom opens the conversation by expressing a desire for a more intimate relationship with the family. 'Welcome,' replies the father; 'and I, in turn, require a thousand piastres of you as a dowry.' After a great deal of noisy discussion, he consents to an abatement of 500 or 600 piastres of the sum, and the bargain is concluded. This is the signal for great rejoicings and the young men of the party amuse themselves with various games and trials of skill, shooting at an ibex head set over the tent door as a mark, being one of the most favorite pastimes. The public notary of the tribe is then called in; he takes a piece of herb and wraps it up in the turban of the intending bridegroom. Taking both of their hands in his own, he places the folded turban between them, and, pressing them closely together, addresses the father of the bride: 'Are you willing to give your daughter in marriage to such an one,' to which he replies: 'I am.' The bridegroom is asked: 'Do you take the girl to wife for better or worse?' On his replying, 'I do take her,' the notary says: 'If you ill-treat her or stint her in food or raiment, the sin be on your own neck.' The questions and answers are repeated three times, and the betrothal is then considered complete. The girl herself is kept until this time, in ignorance of the transaction, and, should she get an inkling of it, it is considered etiquette for her to make a show of escaping to the mountains.

"When she returns in the evening from tending the flocks, and sits down in her father's tent, they place incense on some lighted embers behind her, and fumigate her surreptitiously as a protection against the evil eye. At this moment the notary comes stealthily behind her with the bridegroom's mantle in his hand, which he suddenly throws over her, exclaiming: 'The name of God be with thee! None shall take thee but such an one,' naming her intended husband. Thereupon the girl starts up and tries to escape, calling upon her father and mother for help, with loud cries and shrieks; but she is seized by the women who have collected round her, while they repeat the notary's words in noisy chorus, and utter the shrill cries, called Zogharit! A tent is next erected for her in front of her father's habitation, to which she is conducted, and then sprinkled with the blood of sheep, sacrificed for the occasion. Here she remains for three days, at the end of which time she is conducted by a procession of women to 'a spring of living water,' and after performing her ablutions, is led home to the house of her husband, who makes a great feast in her honor. The neighbors also sacrifice a sheep as a contribution to the entertainment, and receive, as well as the women who have assisted in the ceremony, a trifling present in money from the father of the bride. When a girl who has bestowed her affection on the man of her choice, is compelled by her friends to espouse another, she takes advantage of the three days' grace allowed her, to escape to the tents of some of the neighbors, and throwing herself upon their protection, refuses to leave until the unwelcome suitor relinquishes his claim, and an arrangement entered into between the lover and her relatives. Two girls who were to be married to men they did not like, escaped to the mountains and perished of hunger, rather than prove faithless to their lovers."

The usual mode, however, among the Indians, of obtaining a wife, is by purchase. It is alleged, by those who know, that when an Indian maiden falls in love with a white man, which is sometimes the case, her love is more ardent and more lasting than when she gives her heart to one of her own tribe. It is a historical fact, that several Indian women have committed suicide because they were not permitted to marry white men, whom they devotedly loved.

The Indians have very few gambling games. One, however, resembles our game of dice, and is largely indulged in. It consists of plum stones, painted black on one side and red on the other. They are placed in a dish and are thrown up like our dice. Hennepin says: "There are some so given to this game that they will gamble away their coats. Those who conduct the game, cry at the top of their voices when they rattle the plates, and they strike their shoulders so hard as to leave them all black with the blows." The game is something like "keno."

All Indians are susceptible to kindness as well as revenge. Charka, who attached himself to George H. Spencer, a trader on the frontier, saved his life at the beginning of a Sioux outbreak, at the risk of his own. Amid the bullets of his red brothers and the burning timbers of the building which the savages had fired, he boldly confronted the infuriated demons and his white friend was saved from death, after having been shot through the lungs. So, too, of Other-Day, a good Indian, who interfered in behalf of the whites during the massacre and saved nearly a hundred lives. But, at the same time they remember a wrong.

An Indian was in the habit of coming to a trapper's camp and begging for food. One day he made his appearance as usual, when the trapper, out of all patience with him, took from his pot over a gallon of hot bean soup, which he had just made, and pouring the whole of it into a tin pan, told the Indian to eat, at the same time he brought his gun to bear upon his head and assured him that if he didn't eat all he would blow his brains out! The Indian tugged, and sweated, and munched, and gulped, and moaned, and stretched, until the whole gallon was gone, when he took his departure and was never known to come to that camp again. Some time after this, the trapper became lost in a terrible snow storm, and tired and weary, and hungry, he wandered around until he struck an Indian tepee, and on entering, he found he was in the presence of his lately insulted guest; but hunger was superior to good manners, or even ordinary discretion, so he asked for something to eat, when the Indian brought him a large dish of maple sugar, and seizing his gun, told him if he did not eat every bit of it he would kill him. Fortunately the trapper's appetite was ravenously good, and he got away with most of it, but found it extremely hard to get to the end. He pleaded with the Indian to let him off, but it was no use. "Paleface make Indian eat hot soup; Indian make paleface eat sugar, or paleface dies!" So the poor trapper struggled through his bountiful repast, and more dead than alive, left the tepee impressed with the conviction that it was "more blessed to give than receive," especially when a bushel of sugar was crowded down his throat at the end of a loaded gun, held firmly in the hands of a defiant, revengeful Indian!

The real, genuine amusement of the Indian, is his various dances. He has the Sun Dance, the Dog Dance, the Beggar Dance, the Bear Dance, the Sacred Dance, the Medicine Dance, the War Dance, and many other dances too numerous to recapitulate.

Long, describing his expedition in 1817, writes;

"When we hove in sight, the Indians were engaged in a ceremony called the Bear Dance, a ceremony which they are in the habit of performing when any young man is desirous of bring himself into particular notice, and is considered a kind of initiation into the state of manhood. There was a kind of flag made of fawn skin dressed with the hair on, suspended on a pole. Upon the flesh side of it were drawn certain figures, indicative of the dream which it is necessary the young man should have dreamed before he can be considered a proper canditate for this kind of initiation; with this a pipe was suspended by way of sacrifice. Two arrows were stuck up at the foot of the pole, and fragments of painted feathers, etc., were strewn about the ground near it. These pertained to the religious rites attending the ceremony, which consists in bewailing and self-mortification, that the Good Spirit may be induced to pity them and succor their undertaking. Of course, all this time the dance is going on.

"At the distance of two or three hundred yards from the flag, is an excavation, which they call the Bear's hole, prepared for the occasion. It is about two feet deep, leading across it at right angles. The young hero of the farce, places himself in this hole, to be hunted by the rest of the young men, all of whom, on this occasion, are dressed in their best attire and painted in their neatest style. The hunters approach the hole in the direction of one of the ditches, and discharge their guns, which were previously loaded for the purpose with blank cartridges, at the one who acts the part of the bear; whereupon he leaps from his den, having a hoop in each hand and a wooden lance, the hoop serving as fore feet to aid him in characterizing his part, and his lance to defend himself from his assailants. Thus accoutred, he dances round the place, exhibiting various feats of activity, while the other Indians pursue him and endeavor to trap him, as he attempts to return to his den, to effect which, he is privileged to use any violence he pleases with impunity against his assailants, and even to taking the life of any of them.

"This part of the ceremony is performed three times, that the bear may escape from his den and return to it again through three of the avenues communicating with it. On being hunted from the fourth or last avenue, the bear must make his escape through all his pursuers, if possible, and flee to the woods, where he is to remain through the day. This, however, is seldom or never accomplished, as all the young men exert themselves to the utmost in order to trap him. When caught, he must retire to a lodge erected for his reception in the field, from all society through the day, except one of his particular friends whom he is allowed to take with him as an attendant. Here he smokes and performs various other rites which superstition has led the Indian to believe are sacred. After this ceremony is ended, the young Indian is considered qualified to act any part as an efficient member of their community. The Indian who catches the bear is promoted on the first suitable occasion."

The Dog Dance is only a solid feast, being a "flow of soul" with very little reason. Dog meat is held in great esteem, and hence a dog feast brings out the finest qualities of the Indian's appetite. It is really a time of gayety, and the dance indicates a good time generally.

The War Dance is, perhaps, in one sense, the most horrible of all the dances. A pole is erected, on which are hung the scalps of the enemy, and around which the warriors, profusely painted, dance more energetically than on any other occasion. They form a ring, and in the midst of this ring are the musicians with their drums, who commence beating them slowly, and the Indians then inaugurate their peculiar hops, ever and anon uttering their "hos" and "hi-yis," increasing their motions constantly as they pass round in a circle. Then the drums beat faster, and the warriors dance faster, and their yells become louder, until, when, in a state of terrible frenzy, their eyes glitter, their faces become hideous, and they brandish their knives and tomahawks in close proximity to the brains of their companions, seemingly to almost strike them in their wild and determined actions. Their war-whoops now become simply terrific! They increase the rapidity of their movements! They yell, they wiggle, they throw their arms in the air, and on a moonlight night present all the features of Pandemonium broke loose. This is kept up until nature is completely exhausted, when some one of the warriors steps into the ring and tells what he has done, and what he intends to do, climbing up into the grandiloquent style, being loudly cheered by his companions; and then the dance is over.

The Beggar Dance is peculiar to itself and has considerable significance. The Indians gather about in a dejected manner, and the drum begins its slow, monotonous tones, at the same time the Indians begin to bob up and down, as though one leg was shorter than the other; then the dance increases in earnestness, and the Indians divest themselves of their clothing, first throwing off blankets, then other garments; finally they are almost in a state of nudity. Some Indians who visited my camp and performed this dance, were only prevented from divesting themselves of all their garments, or such as they had on, by my timely interruption in arresting their intentions by having placed in their midst two sacks of flour and an abundance of tobacco. When once supplied they slowly dance until their clothing is replaced, and then gently move away, being always sure of taking their presents with them.

The most sickening of all is the Sun Dance. An unknown writer, who is well posted, has described it so well and so accurately that I append his account:

"The ceremony begins at sunrise and lasts till sundown. During all this time the candidate for honors has to look straight at the sun and dance without any interruption, except to take an occasional puff at the pipe, handed him by the Medicine man. The relatives of the victim sit around the circle, beat the drum—a tin kettle covered with buckskin—and sing of the deeds of great warriors, in order to stimulate to great exertion and pluck, for such is indeed needed by the poor devil during this trying ordeal. Many of the young men faint away during the dance and fail to graduate. The ceremony is as follows:

"There are long strings of rawhide or rope tied to a high, upright pole or tree, upon which the scalps of slaughtered enemies, buffalo skulls, skunk's tails and medicine bags are fastened. The victim takes his position within convenient proximity to the pole, when the Medicine man, with a large double-edged knife or arrowhead, makes two parallel slits in the skin, then runs the sharp point of a stick of wood about four inches long, into one of the slits or cuts, underneath the sinews and out of the other slit or cut. The ends of this stick of wood are then fastened to the strings. This process is inflicted in four places upon the breast and shoulders of the aspirant, who then commences dancing and turning himself around and about, occasionally throwing the whole weight of his body upon the stirrup by which he hangs suspended, dangling and swinging in the air, with the sole object of succeeding, at the earliest possible moment, of tearing out the stitches, sinews and all. As soon as this is accomplished—usually before sundown—the successful graduate is declared a great warrior, and he is given many presents, consisting of guns, pistols, horses, buffalo robes, calico and rings." It is a sickening sight, and partakes of the quintessence of barbarism.

GENERAL GEORGE A. CUSTER.

KILLED IN THE INDIAN FIGHT WITH SITTING BULL.

AS this gallant soldier was engaged for some years in successfully fighting the Indians on our frontier and finally lost his life in the last great Indian battle on the American continent, it seems proper that I should briefly inform the reader who this hero was, and how he became the terror of the red men of the plains. He was the son of a hard-working Ohio farmer, active, bright, amiable, with a fair English education, and who at the age of sixteen years, taught school in his native town. Once determined to go to West Point, he applied to the member of Congress from his own district, and although unsupported by outside influences, he succeeded in gaining the position. His record at the Academy was not a brilliant one, nor was his behavior of the "goody-goody" style, for he was full of mischief and hated restraint. He graduated at the foot of a class of thirty-four. At the breaking out of the rebellion, Custer was ordered to report to General Scott, and when active military events followed he was put on duty with the army which was ingloriously defeated at Bull Run. He was on the staff of several Generals, but finally took his position at the head of a cavalry regiment, and here is where he exhibited those grand traits of character which made him the Marshall Ney of the American army. Nothing seemed to daunt or check him. He swept down upon the foe with the impetuosity of a whirlwind, and the southern soldiers cowered before his victorious troops. With his long, flowing hair hanging down his shoulders, his slouch hat, his embroidered pants, set off with gold; his bright-colored shirt and necktie, he rode at the head of his column and inspired the greatest confidence in his men, so that they, partaking of the leader's spirit, never faltered in the discharge of their duty and never lost a battle.

For one of his heroic and daring achievements, wherein the confederated forces were driven back in confusion, he was promoted from a first lieutenant to a brigadier-general, and, from that time onward, he rapidly ascended the military ladder, until he reached the topmost round—a major-general—and this at the early age of twenty-six years! What is remarkable is the fact, that, amid all the dangers of war—wild, horrible, and terrific—he was only wounded once. One of the last actions in which General Custer was engaged, while fighting for the Union, was his attack upon General Lee's army, and this, with the solid gleaming bayonets of our infantry under the leadership of Sheridan, brought out the white flag, the enemy surrendered, and the war was brought to a close.

In 1867 Custer was ordered to enter the field in pursuit of the Indians, or, rather, at this period, he became identified with the military movements which were then projected for the defense of the frontier. Strong, self-reliant, self-willed, disgusted with restraint, he left Fort Wallace without orders, and, it is alleged, made a journey on private business, for which he was court-marshaled, with suspension of pay and rank for one year, at the end of which time he was recalled into active service, and from thence onward to the period of his death, he became a marked character among the many eminent generals who have conducted our Indian campaigns.

In his onslaughts, in the far West, Custer never stopped to think. His idea was—"Go in and clean them out; they are only Indians!" This is illustrated in his stealthly attack upon an Indian village, where Black Kettle, the chief, was killed, whom General Harney and Colonel Boon declared was as good a friend of the United States as they were. Had Custer paused a moment, this noble old Indian's life might have been saved. But the peculiarities of the boy were well demonstrated in the growth of the man, and this element of character finally cost him his life. In 1873, General Custer came to the new Northwest and with troops escorted the engineers and surveyors of the Northern Pacific railroad into the Yellowstone valley. Here he became acquainted with the fact, that an Indian had killed two elderly men of the expedition, and he had him arrested, and he was imprisoned in Fort Lincoln, where he confessed the deed. His name was Rain-in-the-Face, and he subsequently escaped from the fort, joined the forces of Sitting Bull, and what is singular, on the hotly-contested battle-field, avenged himself by killing the great white chief! And such is fate! After his expedition to the Yellowstone valley, Custer was ordered to proceed to the Black Hills, where he located his troops in a place that now bears his name; and then, following this, he was delegated, by General Terry, to take his seventh cavalry regiment and follow the trail of Sitting Bull, so that three bodies of troops, moving from different directions, might encompass the savages and destroy them, but how he performed this part of his last march I shall reserve for my article on the final great Indian battle on the western plains.

The following from the pen of a gentleman who accompanied General Custer on his Yellowstone expedition, gives a more excellent insight into the man's character, than anything I have seen, and with it I conclude my notice of this remarkable military hero, only regretting that he could not have lived to a hale and hearty old age.

"General Custer was a born cavalry man. He was never more in his element than when mounted on Danby, his favorite horse, and riding at the head of his regiment. He was the personification of bravery and dash. If he had only added discretion to his valor, he would have been a perfect soldier. His impetuosity often ran away with his judgment. He was impatient of control. He liked to act independently of others, and take all the risk and all the glory to himself. He frequently got himself into trouble by assuming more authority than really belonged to his rank. From the time when he entered West Point, to the day when he fell on the Big Horn, he was accustomed to take just as much liberty as he was entitled to. For this reason, Custer worked most easily and effectively when under general orders, when not hampered by special instructions, or his success made dependent on anybody else. General Terry understood his man, when, in the order directing him to march up the Rosebud, he very liberally said: 'The Department Commander places too much confidence in your zeal, energy and ability to wish to impose upon you precise orders which might hamper your actions when nearly in contact with the enemy.'

But General Terry did not understand Custer if he thought he would wait for Gibbon's support before attacking an Indian village. Undoubtedly he ought to have done this; but with his native impetuosity, his reckless daring, his confidence in his own regiment, which had never failed him, and his love of public approval, Custer could no more help charging this Indian camp, than he could help charging just so many buffaloes. He had never learned to spell the word 'defeat;' he knew nothing but success, and if he had met the Indians on the open prairie, success would undoubtedly have been his; for no body of Indians could stand the charge of the seventh cavalry, when it swept over the plains like a whirlwind.

"With all his bravery and self-reliance, his love of indepedent action, Custer was more dependent than most men, on the kind approval of his fellows. He was even vain; he loved display in dress and in action. He would pay forty dollars for a pair of trooper boots to wear on parade and have everything else in keeping. On the Yellowstone expedition he wore a bright red shirt which made him the best mark for a rifle of any man in the regiment. On the next campaign he appeared in a buckskin suit. He formerly wore his hair very long, letting it fall in a heavy mass upon his shoulders, but cut it off before going out to the Black Hills, producing quite a change in his appearance. But if vain and ambitious, Custer had none of those great vices which are common and so distressing in the army. He never touched liquor in any form; he did not smoke, or chew, or gamble. He was a man of great energy and remarkable endurance. When he set out to reach a certain point at a certain time, you could be sure that he would be there if he killed every horse in the command. He was sometimes too severe in enforcing marches, but he never seemed to get tired himself and he never expected his men to get so. Whatever he did, he did thoroughly. He would overshoot the mark, but never fall short of it. He fretted in garrison sometimes, because it was too inactive; but he found an outlet here for his energies in writing articles for the press.

"He had a remarkable memory. He would recall, in its proper order, every detail of any action, no matter how remote, of which he was a participant. As he was apt to overdo in action, so he was apt to exaggerate in statement, not from any willful disregard of the truth, but because he saw things bigger than they really were. He did not distort the truth; he magnified it. He took rose-colored views of everything. He had a historical memory, but not a historical mind. He was no philospher; could read off from his mind better than he could analyze or mass them. He was not a student, or a deep thinker. He loved to take part in events rather than to brood over them. He was fond of fun; genial and pleasant in his manners; a loving and devoted husband. He had many most excellent traits of character which will live long after the memories of other men are forgotten."

MAJOR GENERAL TA-TON-KA-I-G-O-TON-KA; OR, SITTING BULL.

THIS Indian deserves the rank of Major General in the army of the savages, for, of all the chiefs, he was the most implacable, the most unrelenting, the most hostile, the most sagacious, and the most desperate foe of the whites of any chief of modern times. He never assented to the control of the United States Government over the people, but persistently fought our troops whenever they came in his way. He did, however, agree to make a treaty with the good Father De Smet, but the treaty was violated. He claimed that the country belonged to the Indians; that they had a right to hunt and fish wherever they pleased; that the white man had wronged them; and thus appealing to the feelings of the younger portion of his race, induced a large number to follow him, and for twenty years carried on his war, until he finally surrendered to the United States forces, on the 19th of July, 1881.

From the earliest history of the man, down to the time he yielded his power, he had been a vindictive and determined enemy of the whites. His successful raids and savage victories; his unfaltering purposes to harrass, rob and kill the settlers; his undaunted courage and wily reasoning; his successful battles and wise counsels, soon elevated him to the highest pitch of a leading and powerful chief, and he gathered about him men of the same peculiar cast of mind, and continued to march forth to success and to victory, until his name became well known in every part of this country and in Europe. These successes, on the part of Sitting Bull, inspired the Indian heart, so that many who were living on the bounty of the Government at the various agencies, left and joined his forces, and hence he was a constant source of disturbance, even outside of his own immediate command. Indians who were peacefully inclined, flocked to his ranks, and for a time he put at defiance that portion of the army of the United States then operating on our frontier.

His influence had become so great and was working such deleterious effect among the agency Indians, that finally the Department at Washington was obliged to take prompt measures to prevent a general outbreak among the friendly Indian tribes, and to this end Sitting Bull and his followers were ordered to come in on to the Reservation, or they would fall under the control of the military power. Sitting Bull laughed at these commands of the Indian Department, and still continued his raids; and then followed the campaign of 1876, inaugurated by General Sheridan, wherein three powerful columns of troops were to move simultaneously upon the enemy and force them either into civilization or extermination. In the attempt to carry out this movement, which was a wise one, it will be remembered General Crooks was repulsed, and General Custer, in his eagerness to make an attack without proper support, which could have been obtained, brought on a fight in which he and his men were all killed, leaving Sitting Bull and his warriors complete masters of the field. No such Indian battle was ever known before in this country; and such a complete Indian victory has no parallel in history, and we are forced to the conclusion that it could have been avoided had General Custer not been misled as to the number of Indians in the village, or had he refrained from an attack, or had he promptly informed General Terry when he first discovered the Indian camp, and waited for his support.

After this battle the savages crossed into Canada, and, notwithstanding there were several Indian fights on this side of the boundary line subsequently, yet Sitting Bull took no part in them for a year. Then the old chieftain began again to commit depredations among the Americans, and, finally a commissioner was appointed by the United States Government to cross the line and try to effect, by diplomacy, what had failed by force of arms. In the meantime Sitting Bull's forces had greatly decreased by the return of the outlaws back into the agencies whence they originally had come; and here they were fed and petted again by a great Government, which had failed to subdue them, and which, when these renegades were in its power, had failed to punish them. Through the intercession of British officers, the Peace Commissioners were ushered into the presence of the august chieftain, who disdainfully refused to shake hands with them, and arrogantly demanded that they should come out from behind the table they were sitting around, and speak the truth to his chiefs. No such audacity was ever shown before in the history of the Indian race; and then, after all the humiliating promises made by the Government, Major-general Sitting Bull sneeringly rejected every overture for peace, and the Commission, having marched up the hill, marched down again, and the grim old soldier quietly smoked his pipe inside of the walls of his greasy tepee.

Matters now continued quiet with Sitting Bull for nearly one year and a half, when, in 1879, he broke out again and commenced his depredations upon the settlers. He was met by General Miles and a battle ensued, Sitting Bull being in command in person, but fearing that the whites would be reinforced, he wisely withdrew his warriors and retreated to the British possessions, where he remained peacefully until he gave up his arms to the American forces. Then followed the surrender of Rain-in-the-Face, Crow Wing, Chief Gaul, and many thousand Indians, leaving Sitting Bull with only a few disheartened warriors, and finally, sullenly and in a defiant manner, he succumbed to the inevitable march of the white race, came within our lines and everybody felt better and breathed freer when he surrendered.

J. E. Walker, Esq., who witnessed the capitulation of Sitting Bull, says:

"With the last remnant of his people, some two hundred souls, old men, women and children, the old war-chief arrived at Fort Buford, Dakota, at noon on July 19, 1881. At the head of the mournful cortege rode Sitting Bull, Four Horns, Red Thunder, and other sub-chiefs on their ponies, and following came six army wagons loaded with the squaws and children, and behind them came some twenty-five Red river carts containing their baggage. They presented a forlorn and pitiful appearance, the great Sitting Bull himself being very dirty and very hungry; his face wearing a sullen, bull-dog expression; his dress and appearance bearing marks of the hardships and destitution he had recently experienced. Yet, until called upon to surrender his arms, he preserved under this the most trying ordeal to a savage, a dignified and unbroken silence. Thus ended the Indian war in the Northwest—the closing of the five years' campaign against the most remarkable Indian leader of modern times.

"While the last act of the drama, the final scene in Sitting Bull's career as a warrior, was enacted at noon, July 20, 1881, and when, by the hand of his little son, he delivered up the rifle he had carried throughout so many bloody fields, the great chieftan spoke as follows: 'I surrender this rifle to you through my young son, whom I now desire to teach in this manner, that he has become a friend of the American people. I wish him to learn the habits of the whites and to be educated as their sons are educated. I wish it to be remembered that I was the last man of my tribe to surrender my rifle. This boy has given it to you, and he now wants to know how he is going to make a living. Whatever you have to give and whatever you have to say, I would like to receive or hear now, for I don't wish to be kept in darkness longer. I have sent several messengers in here from time to time, but none of them have returned with news. The other chiefs, Crow Wing and Gaul, have not wanted me to come, and I have never received good news from here. I wish now to be allowed to live this side of the line, or the other, as I see fit. I wish to continue my old life of hunting, but would like to be allowed to trade on both sides of the line. This is my country, and I don't want to be compelled to give it up. My heart was very sad at having to leave the mother's country. She has been a friend to me, but I want my children to grow up in my native country, and I wish also to feel that I can visit two of my friends on the other side of the line whenever I wish, and would like to trade with Legare, as he has always been a friend to me. I wish to have all my people live together upon one reservation of our own on the Little Missouri. I left several families at Wood Mountain and between there and Qu'Appelle. I have many people among the Yanktonaise at Poplar Creek, and I wish all of them and those who have gone to Standing Rock, to be collected together upon one reservation. My people have, many of them, been bad. All are good now, that their arms and ponies have been taken from them. (Speaking to the officer:) You own this ground with me, and we must try and help each other. I do not wish to leave here until I get all the people I left behind. I would like to have my daughter, who is now at Fort Yates, sent up here to visit me, as also eight men, and I would like to know that Legare is to be rewarded for his services in bringing me and my people here.'"

Sitting Bull, Rain-in-the-Face, Gaul, Long Dog, Spotted Horn Bull, Eagle, Grey Eagle, Flying By, Crow Eagle and other chiefs of his tribe, with some three thousand of his people, are now at Standing Rock agency, Dakota, on the Missouri river, and thus ends the unparalleled career of this greatest of modern Indian chiefs.

THE LAST GREAT INDIAN BATTLE ON THE AMERICAN CONTINENT.

IN WHICH GENERAL CUSTER LOST HIS LIFE AND SITTING BULL BECAME THE VICTORIOUS CONQUEROR.

"Ye've trailed me through the forests,
Ye've tracked me o'er the plain,
But with your bristling bayonets,
Ye ne'er shall track again."

THE reader who has perused the pages of this book, treating of the lives of General Custer and Sitting Bull, must now be pretty well prepared to learn of the final conflict between two of the most noted warriors of modern times—the one the representative of civilization, the other the representative of barbarism.

As has already been narrated, General Terry sought to mass three columns of troops upon the savages, from three different points, for two reasons: First, to prevent the Indians from escaping; and second to force them to surrender or annihilate them. To this end 2,700 men, divided into three columns of 1,300, 400 and 1,000 each, started out in the year 1876, in pursuit of the savages under Sitting Bull, then supposed to be somewhere in the Yellowstone valley, and numbering about 3,000 warriors. These columns of troops were to gradually encircle the Indians, and to pounce down upon them with such irresistible force as to completely overpower them, General Gibbons coming in from one direction, General Terry from another, and Custer from another. The latter officer was to be at the head of his favorite regiment, the seventh cavalry, consisting of 28 officers and 747 men, then pronounced in splendid condition; and when, therefore, Major Reno came in from his scouting expedition, reporting a heavy Indian trail, ten days old, General Terry decided upon his mode of attack and the disposition of his forces. Custer was to ascend the valley of the Rosebud, turn toward the Little Big Horn river, keeping well to the south, while Gibbons was to cross the Yellowstone at the mouth of Big Horn river, and march up the Big Horn to its junction with the Little Big Horn, to co-operate with Custer.

The general's Indian fighting qualities were so well known to Terry, that in giving his orders to him, he distinctly stated—"that he would not impose upon him precise orders which might hamper his actions when nearly in contact with the enemy;" and hence I think herein was the great mistake of the expedition, for, had Terry given *positive* instructions to Custer, first to hunt out the Indians, then to inform him where they were, then to come to a halt and await support, there is no doubt but Custer would be alive to-day, and Sitting Bull would be dwelling in his happy hunting ground, beyond the reach of the white man's bullets. But these orders were not given, for reasons best known to General Terry, and Custer, acting out the impetuous impulsiveness of his nature, after discovering the Indians, ordered Major Reno, with three companies, to cross the Rosebud river on the left, attack the enemy in the rear, while he, with five companies, numbering upwards of three hundred men, would move forward on the right and make an attack in front. Two other companies were ordered to make a detour south of Reno. In the meantime General Terry, with his cavalry and the battery, had pushed on with the hope of opening up communication with Custer, as Terry no doubt fully believed that Custer would refrain from making an attack on the Indians village until he (Terry) was within supporting distance, and he was hurrying forward to effect this result, when three Crow Indians, who started out with Custer's regiment, came into camp and reported that a battle had been fought and the Indians were killing white men in great numbers.

It seems that Major Reno entered the woods on the left of the Rosebud and made the attack as ordered, but he was overpowered by great numbers of Indians, and finally retreated across the river under a galling fire, and gained a rise of ground, where he rapidly threw up retrenchments and put himself on the defensive. The other two companies from the south soon joined him, and here a desperate effort was made by the enemy to dislodge him, but without success. While this was going on, General Custer had passed down the north banks of the river, and had made two unsuccessful attempts to cross it, but was repulsed by the Indians, who outnumbered him some fifteen to one, and after stubbornly contesting this point, he fell back to a small eminence, and there the battle raged most terrifically. Soldiers and horses fell from the unerring bullets of the Indians like wheat under the stroke of the scythe. The brave men, led by their brave but deceived leader, continued to close up the gaps made by the enemy, until not a living soul was left upon the field! All was still! All was gone! Three hundred men! hundreds of horses! the most gallant cavalry officer America ever produced, had passed out of life, out of activity, out of reality, down into the shadow of death!

Sitting Bull and his chiefs, satiated with the copious blood of the pale faces, and fearful of the advancing troops, called off their men from any further attack on Reno; gathered up their scattered village and moved outside of the limits of harm, while Terry, coming up with his reserved forces, found only a beseiged camp (Reno's), a silent battle field, mutiliated bodies, an Indian victory, a triumphant chief moving securely outside of the range of civilized guns, and gloating over the ruin he had made!

Curley, a Crow Indian, who was with Custer, two other scouts, and "Comanche," one of the officers' horses, were the only living beings and creatures that escaped from that doomed battle field. Curley gives his story as follows:

"Custer kept down the river on the north bank four miles, after Reno had crossed to the south side above. Thought Reno would drive down the valley to attack the village at the upper end, while he (Custer), would go in at the lower end. Custer had to advance further down the river and further away from Reno than he wished, on account of the steep bank along the north side; but at last he found a ford and dashed for it. The Indians met him and poured in a heavy fire from across the narrow river. Custer dismounted to fight on foot, but could not get his skirmishers over the stream. Meantime hundreds of Indians on foot and on ponies, rushed over the river, which was only about three feet deep, and filled the ravine on each side of Custer's men. Custer then fell back to some high ground behind him and seized the ravines in his immediate vicinity. The Indians completely surrounded Custer, and poured in a terrible fire on all sides. They charged Custer on foot in vast numbers, but were again and again driven back.

"The fight began about two o'clock and lasted almost until the sun went down over the hills. The men fought desperately, and after the ammunition in their belts was exhausted, went to their saddle-bags, got more, and continued the fight. Custer lived until nearly all his men had been killed or wounded, and went about encouraging his soldiers to fight on. He got a shot in the left side and sat down with his pistol in his hand. Another shot struck Custer in the breast, and he fell over. The last officer killed was a man who rode a white horse.

"When he saw Custer hopelessly surrounded, he watched his opportunity, got a Sioux blanket, put it on and worked up a ravine, and when the Sioux charged, he got among them and they did not know him from one of their own men. There were some mounted Sioux, and seeing one fall, he ran to him, mounted his pony and galloped down as if going toward the white men, but went up a ravine and got away. As he rode off he saw when nearly a mile from the battle field, a dozen or more soldiers in a ravine fighting with Sioux all around them. He thinks all were killed, as they were outnumbered five to one and apparently dismounted. The battle was desperate in the extreme, and more Indians than white men must have been killed."

Kill Eagle, who was in Sitting Bull's camp at the time of the battle, describes the village as six miles long and one wide. He then speaks of Custer's approach and fight, with its tragic details as an anwilling spectator rather than as a participant, who, during its progress, remained quietly in his lodge in the center of the Indian village. The fight with Reno commenced about noon, the Indians all rushing to oppose his advance until the approach of Custer toward the end of the village was announced, when the wildest confusion prevailed throughout the camp. Lodges were struck and preparation made for instant fight. Vast numbers of Indians left Reno's front and hastened to the assistance of their red brethren engaged with Custer, who was steadily forced back and surrounded until all were swept from the field by the repeated charges of the Indians.

He describes the firing at this point as simply terrific, and illustrated its force by clapping his hands together with great rapidity and regularity. Then came a lull in the fearful storm of iron and hail, and his hands were still again. The storm beat fast and furious, as the thought of some loved one nerved the arm of each contending trooper. Then the movement of his hands slackened and gradually grew more feeble. A few scattering shakes, like the rain upon a window-pane, and then the movement ceased, as the last of Custer's band of heroes went down with the setting sun.

It was dark when the successful Indians returned to camp, littered with their dead and wounded. "We have killed them all," they said; "put up your lodges where they are." They had just begun to fix their lodges that evening, when a report came that troops were coming from toward the mouth of the creek. When this report came, after dark, the lodges were all taken down, and the Indians started up the creek. It was not to the Indians a bloodless victory. Fourteen had fallen in front of Reno, thirty-nine went down with Custer, and fourteen were dead in camp. Over one hundred were wounded. There were no white men among the Indian forces, in the fight, or on the field. The bugle calls were sounded by an Indian. No prisoners were taken. The troops were all killed on the east side; none crossed the river.

Little Buck Elk was present at the fight and said: "The Indians were as thick as bees and there were so many of them that they could not all take part. The soldiers were all brave men and fought well; some of them, when they found themselves surrounded and overpowered, broke through the lines and tried to make their escape, but were pursued and killed miles from the battle-field. The Indians captured six battle flags. No soldiers were taken alive, but after the fight the women went among the dead bodies and robbed and multilated them."

It is a mistaken idea that Indians do not understand the paraphernalia of war. They have out their spies, their scouts and their skirmishers, and are generally well posted on the movements of their enemy. For instance, a spy overlooking the rendezvous of soldiers, conveys the information by running to another Indian stationed a certain distance from him, of how many troops there are, etc., and he, in turn, runs to another, and so on, until the news reaches the camp of the chief, though it may be many miles away. Then they form coalition with the other bands, as in the case of the Custer fight, and on the battle field they have signs by which they move their men, one of which is the "Hiyi-yis" of their chiefs which means "follow us." Again they convey significant signs great distances, both by smoke and by the reflection of the looking glass, or by some bright metal.

The great major-general of the Sioux army, Sitting Bull, was well informed as to the action of Terry's soldiers, long before they left for an attack, and as he had been drawing from the agency Indians, not only men but means to prosecute the war, and had made alliances with other bands, he was well prepared to meet the issue; and Custer, instead of confronting 2,000 warriors, as he expected to, fell into the hands of 5,000! If General Terry had not come up just as he did, Reno and his men would have shared the same fate as Custer, because the Indians would have pitched their tepees near the battle-field and in the morning would have renewed the attack and with entire success. Hearing that reinforcements were coming to the whites, they moved away and finally crossed into the British possessions.

Taken all together history will point to this as the greatest Indian battle on American soil, and especially so, as involving the gallant fighting characteristics of two of the greatest warriors of the nineteenth century, the one nobly and heroically meeting his death upon the battle-field, against superior numbers, the other now a captive in the hands of the whites, against whom he had so long and so successfully fought.

Now, after all this, if Major-General Sitting Bull desires civilization for his people—desires education for his children—desires sincerely to adopt the habits of the whites, let us give him the helping hand. He was great in his last battle, and he may yet prove greater still in elevating his own race.

SITTING BULL'S FIRST VISIT TO CIVILIZATION.

STRANGE events transpire in all phases of life. In the eternal revolution of the wheel of time, even the lion and the lamb will lie down together, and the day is rapidly approaching when Barbarism and Civilization will shake hands over a common cause, a common destiny, a common country. A few years ago, and the great Indian war chief, Sitting Bull, was the unrelenting, implacable enemy of the whites. He turned his back upon civilization; scorned all overtures for peace, except in one instance, and feeling that he had been wronged, he marshaled his forces and combatted every opposing power. He was an untutored child of nature; honestly believed that the whites had wronged him, and in some respects they had, and thus feeling, he expected to live and to die, as it were, an outlaw. He was moving with his warriors toward the Canadian line, where he intended to live the remainder of his days, when, of a sudden, he was attacked by Custer, and in the engagement that followed, not a white soldier of over three hundred was left to tell the story of that dreadful battle. He crossed the line. Negotiations followed. Efforts were made to bring Sitting Bull within the power of the United States. He refused to come, and remained on Canadian soil until his leading chiefs consented to surrender, and after many of them had done so, he finally yielded and came within the American lines. Only on one occasion besides this did Sitting Bull assent to be a representative to a treaty with the whites, and that was about the country including the Black Hills, and as this treaty was not respected, of course he felt indignant, and continued to feel indignant until his surrender to the United States forces, as narrated in these pages. At the council held by the good Father De Smet, Sitting Bull came forward and said:

SPEECH OF SITTING BULL.

"Father, you pray to the Great Spirit for us, and I thank you. I will and I have often besought the kindness of the Great Spirit, but never have I done so more earnestly than to-day, that our words may be heard above and to all quarters of the earth. When I first saw you coming, I had evil thoughts and my heart beat, caused by the remembrance of the past. But I bade it be still, and it was so; when I shook hands with you, my comrade, and my sister, in the prairie, I felt a change and hardly knew what to say, but my heart was glad and quickly formed a decision. I am and I have always been a fool and a warrior. My people caused me to be so. They have been confused and troubled for several years past, and they look upon their troubles as coming from the whites, and became crazy as it were and pushed me forward. I have led them for the past four years in bad deeds. The fault is their's as much as mine. I will now say in their hearing, welcome, father, messenger of peace, and I hope quiet and more to our country, As I am not full of words, I will now thank you in the presence of our chiefs and braves for your kindness, and I accept the tobacco as a token of peace, trusting that you will always continue to wish us well. I have now told you all, and all is said that can be said. Some of my people will return with you to meet the chiefs of our great father, who are sent to make peace. I hope it will be all accomplished and whatever is done by them I will accept and remain ever a friend to the whites."

After shaking hands with us all he turned to the crowd and asked them if they had heard his words. "How! how!" ran through the crowd. A moment after he returned and said he had forgotten three things. He wished all to know that he did not propose to sell any part of his country, nor did he wish the whites to cut his timber along the Missouri, and especially the oaks. He was particularly fond of looking at the little groves of oaks and had a reverence for them. They had withstood the wintry storms and summer blasts and, not unlike themselves, seemed to flourish by them. His last request was that the forts, peopled with soldiers, should be abandoned, as there was no greater source of grievance to his people. With applause from young and old he took his seat.

SITTING BULL IN SAINT PAUL, MINNESOTA.

The person who conceived the excellent idea of introducing Sitting Bull for the first time to civilization, was Major James McLaughlin, Indian agent at Standing Rock, and in this conception he carried out a bold idea, the results of which will prove greatly beneficial to the Indian tribes over which Sitting Bull has an influence. Like the old Roman soldier, Bull could say—"*veni, vidi, vici*"—"I came, I saw, I conquered—not armies of men; not a chieftain of the Great Father, or a foe of my own race; but I conquered my own prejudices and the prejudices of the white people, and saw—not emblems of war, or revenge, or blood, or carnage, but evidences of peace, of harmony, of industry, commerce, schools, churches, kindness, friends, civilization. I came among a people who had been taught to believe that I was the most brutal savage on the face of the earth, and I must confess I felt for a moment uneasy as to my personal safety, but the great heart of the paleface made my own heart quiet and grateful for its generosity and magnanimity, and I went back to my people deeply impressed with the vastness of the white race and the power of civilization." Such was the feeling of this great uncivilized warrior after he had seen civilization for the first time in his life, and on returning to Standing Rock, where his people are gathered, he gave them such a glowing account of what he had seen, that a number of the chiefs would not believe him, and others have become so deeply interested in the elevation of their race that they have signified their desires to abandon barbarism and adopt the modes and the habits of the whites. So much for Sitting Bull's visit.

WHEN AND WHERE BORN—ORIGIN OF NAME.

Ta-ton-ka-i-g-o-ton-ka, or Sitting Bull, was born in 1834, on the banks of the Grand river, within the boundaries of the present Great Sioux Reservation, near the mouth of Stonewall creek, and about forty-five miles southwest from Standing Rock Agency in Dakota Territory. He states that he was born in the spring and is now in his fiftieth year, but he looks much older. His sister, however, who is six years his senior corroborates his statement, and says that he was born fifty winters ago, or in the spring of 1834. He was first named "Wakan-you-najin," — Standing Holy, which name he retained until he was fourteen years old, when his father, whose name was Sitting Bull, took him along with him on the war-path into the Crow country (the inveterate enemies of the Sioux), and he, the fourteen year old boy, counted his first coup or victory, by killing a Crow Indian. After returning to their home, his father *threw away* three ponies in honor of his brave son's achievement, at the same time announcing that he had changed the name of his son from Standing Holy to that of Sitting Bull, bestowing his own name upon him. His father was subsequently killed by the Crows near the forks of Grand river.

In person Sitting Bull is a solidly-built Indian, not quite so tall as an ordinary savage, yet heavier in many respects. His features are strong, and, when he walks, he turns his toes inward, strikes the ground with a heavy, jarring tread, and moves along rapidly, like a man of business. His general look is heavy, while that of Little Crow, the leader of the great Indian outbreak, and Hole-in-the-Day, the great Chippewa chief, were more refined, but, none the less, true Indians. The Dakotas believe that they must imitate their Hay-o-kah, or undemonstrative god, who inculcates the idea that it is not dignified, nor manly, nor great to evince lively emotions of grief or joy, but, under all circumstances, even of torture and death itself, the Indian must show a stoical, impassive face, and, hence, the immovable features of sitting Bull, or any other Indian who lays claim to power among his tribe. It is alleged that Bull is not so able a man in intellect as Gaul, Antelope, and others, but he is very self-willed, one might say obstinate, and here is where he gets his strength and his fame. And yet this very stubbornness of character has made him a name second to no other chief in Indian history, as the same element of character made Grant the greatest warrior of modern times.

Major McLaughlin and his two little sons (one acting as interpreter), with Sitting Bull, One Bull and others arrived at St. Paul, Minnesota, on March 14, 1884, and in consequence of the great crowd at the depot, gathered to see the famous Unkapapa, he took a hack to one of our principal hotels. That evening was spent by the chief in examining type setting, newspaper making, telegraphing, telephoning, steam-heating, etc., in which he took great interest. The next day he investigated several grocery and commission houses, saw the process of coffee roasting and grinding, and for the first time rode in an elevator. The next day he called on Bishop Grace, and talked for some time in his own tongue, with Father Ravoux; passed through the cathedral, and the Assumption Catholic churches; visited the State capitol; examined the portraits of the governors; said of General Sibley, "Had hoped to meet him, and was sorry that he must return without seeing him, as he was the true friend of the Indian race, and trusted that the trip South would bring him back strong and healthy again."

He then rode through the city and saw its fine residences and business blocks; returned to the hotel, and on Sunday morning attended mass at the Assumption church; later, saw the action of the fire department, and was so pleased with its workings that the performance was repeated for his benefit, he touching the electric signal for the call. He then, on invitation, visited one of the largest cigar factories in the city, and after witnessing the process of manufacturing the article, was presented with two twelve-inch cigars, made in his presence; went through the public schools; saw 1,000 pupils issue from one building in two minutes after the fire alarm had been given; strolled through a large millinery establishment; opened his eyes very wide when inside of a wholesale boot and shoe manufacturing establishment, especially when his measure was taken and he had a complete pair of shoes made and handed to him, in twenty minutes after the leather had passed into the hands of the first workman. He followed the process all through, and was more astonished at this, than at anything that he had seen that day. He has not worn the shoes yet, but keeps them to show and explain to his visitors how they are made.

He became an Irishman on St. Patrick's day, and attended an entertainment in the evening and made a speech; spent several hours in a wholesale dry goods house; saw a pair of pants made in two minutes; extended his visit to Fort Snelling; dined with his old antagonist, General Terry; graced the Grand Opera house with his presence; was delighted with the play, and especially when the actors took off their wigs; "went through" one of the principal banks; took in his hands a parcel containing $400,000 in United States bonds, and, being uncivilized, he carefully handed it back; shuffled through the post-office; saw the mails, and some of the females; made for the railway offices; attended another theater in the evening; sat for his picture; called on friends of his benefactor, Major McLaughlin; made a tour of the mills at Minneapolis; saw the city, and took the train for home that evening, having been fourteen days from the agency, which was acknowledged by Sitting Bull to be the most pleasant and beneficially spent of any days of his life.

THE MOTIVE FOR VISITING CIVILIZATION.

We learn from Indian Agent McLaughlin, that the object in inducing Sitting Bull and his nephew to visit St. Paul, was to show them the greatness and the power of the whites; to see how they live; the many comforts they enjoy, and to impress upon them the importance of the introduction of industrious habits among the Indians and the education of their children, and great pains were taken to explain to them that all the comforts the whites enjoyed, and every convenience they had, cost labor and thought, and thus seeing all this, it was suggested, would be more convincing than years of theoretical education, and this was deemed especially important in the case of Sitting Bull. It has turned out as was expected. His eyes have been opened by his recent visit to civilization, and it is exhibiting itself in many ways since his return. He is now more ready to believe what he is told him about the whites than formerly. As a great leader his influence is now somewhat limited, and his followers are of the most unenlightened class. Whatever power he has, however, is being turned in the right direction, and his recent trip to the marts of civilization has been largely instrumental in bringing this about. He never tires of talking of what he saw and the kind treatment he received from all whom he met, and no fears need now be entertained of any further trouble from him, or through him among the Sioux. And thus we close an interesting chapter of an interesting chief of an interesting people who are gradually emerging out of barbarism into the full glare of civilization, and we trust, and we have reason to hope, that this little volume has had something to do toward the consummation of so desirable an end.

AN INTERESTING TRIP.

WHERE NO WHITE MAN HAD EVER BEEN BEFORE.

IN the year 1865, when on the north boundary line of the United States, I met an Indian who attached himself to me as my necarnis, or best friend, and who desired that I should go with him some forty miles from that point, to examine what he claimed was a bed of coal; so, asking him how much, and receiving the reply, "$50," I consented to give it, and began preparations for the journey. It was winter, and Vermilion lake was frozen over, so that my "shebang," as I called it, consisting of a horse and covered sled, could easily make the trip. The Indian was to meet me some distance from the camp, so as not to excite the suspicion of our exploring party, and in the morning, bright and early, myself and Porter, the interpreter, started out, and soon Nar-go-ba-da was seen in the distance, awaiting our coming. Indian-like, he wanted a gallon of "scoot-a-wa-boo," or whisky, before he would budge an inch. I positively declined to give him this, but I told him that I would give him a drink then, and as the fatigue of the journey increased, he should have more; so, satisfied, he gave the lead, and we followed. It was a crisp, bright, sharp winter morning, and the wide expanse of the frozen lake stretched out before us. Nar-go-ba-da loomed up ahead; I followed; Porter was behind. When about eight miles from our point of departure, I was startled with the vision behind me of a large body of men and horses following our trail, and the more I looked the more distinct they became.

"Porter! for heaven's sake," I asked, "what is the meaning of that body of men and horses behind us? I thought we were alone on the lake. Look!" Porter looked; the Indian looked; I looked; there the men and horses were, just as I had described them, but I could see a smile play over the features of the Indian and Porter, while on my own were evidences of surprise.

"Who are you! where are they going?" I asked eagerly. By this time Porter had come up, and Nar-go-ba-da had returned from the advance, and as we were then all looking at them I observed that the immense regiment as it were, halted, and when Porter, with his lame leg, moved, I saw one of their men with a lame leg move also, and then I began, as the boy did—"to smell a mice," but what this strange vision was I could not yet comprehend. "Well," said Porter, "Maria." "What do you mean by that?" I asked. "A grand display of our own persons and horse multiplied into hundreds; a reflection of ourselves, produced by the peculiar condition of the atmosphere." Can it be possible that I had been thus deceived? Yes, when we moved, they moved, and what was more convincing to me, was the fact of Porter's game leg, for one of the other party was in the same fix.

These delusions occur quite frequently on this lake, especially on a frosty morning. Some parties have been absolutely frightened by seeing others following them, and have started out on a run—of course the others after them—and have not stopped until they have reached their camp, and then they have turned to find nothing but their own shadows.

Quiet and order being somewhat restored in our ranks

Nar-go-ba-da took the lead, and on we sped over the slight snow which covered the lake. Suddenly our Indian came to a halt, and I with him, and here we found a circle made in the snow, and at a given point in that circle was a mark, indicating at what time and which way a party of trappers had passed that morning, clearly showing the sagacity of the Indian in not only telling time, but also in indicating the points of the compass. Our line of march was as follows: the Indian first, myself and horse next, Porter last. The snow was deep, so we had to keep in the beaten track of the trappers, and thus, in the order named, we pushed on. Presently we heard a loud yell from Nar-go-ba-da. I thought a thousand Indians were on my path, and requested Porter to hurry up, and we together approached the Indian, who, we found, had discovered the hunting ground of his friends, and there lay before us a huge lynx, with a rope around his neck and the other end attached to a long limb of a tree.

The Indian's primitive mode of trapping is interesting, especially when the snow is deep. He first passes over the track of the animal on snow shoes. That night this track freezes. He then gathers small sticks, as an Irish woman would make a hen yard; these sticks he places across the track a foot or two out from it on either side, leaving in the middle and directly where the snow is hard a small aperture, and in this aperture is hung a slipping-noose of fine but very strong twine, the other end tied to a limb of a tree. Now, in the morning the lynx comes out for his breakfast; he trots along down the hardened track; he snuffs the hunter's evening meal; when, all of a sudden, he comes to the little sticks in his path; they look natural enough; he puts his paw to one side; it sinks in the snow; he tries the other side, that sinks; he hesitates; when he sees a small opening and a fine string hanging therein, he tries the snow on either side of the path again; it is too deep; he makes a plunge into the opening, is caught by the slipping-noose around his neck; he pulls, he struggles, he growls, he bites, and the harder he pulls the tighter grows the string around his neck until the fellow is dead. The animal before us was a large, splendid creature, with huge limbs of immense power, a small, round head, and covered with a beautiful garment of winter. This mode of trapping keeps the fur in a fine condition; unpolluted by poison and uninjured by bullets. My necarnis was delighted with the "find," and so on again we pushed in our journey.

We had been traveling about an hour, when again I heard the Indian scream more terribly than ever before, and this time I drew my revolver and called to him to halt, as at the time he was approaching me, and he halted, and I halted, and there we stood looking at each other until Porter came up, when the Indian broke out in the most excited gibberish, the tenor of which was, that he had suddenly approached Spirit Island, where he saw a large ox and a horse appear, and he was greatly alarmed. He had heard of this place but he had never before seen it, and even while he spoke, he pointed to the island, and insisted that the animals were there, he could see them, but we could discover none. The fevered condition of his mind, or of his imagination, had much to do in making it appear to him real, when to us, it was only a myth. And yet, Porter says it is the universal belief of the Indians, especially the Brules in this section, that spirits of Indians, horses, ponies, oxen, etc., inhabit this island.

This second scare over, we again took up our line of march, and, just at sundown, struck the borders of an island, some thirty-five miles from whence we had come. Here a small camp-fire was made on the island, our supper cooked, and early I turned into my covered sled, some three hundred feet from where the Indian and Porter lay. In my sled I had a Henry rifle and two revolvers, and felt pretty safe; and yet I did not like to be so far from my friends. I looked out into the night; the moon was shining brightly; and then, fastening down the covers of my "shebang," I gathered the clothes about me, and was soon in a sweet sleep. About midnight I was awakened by a noise near the sled. To me it seemed like the tread of Indians, and I knew, that if this was the case, there was no hope for me, for they were there for a bad purpose; so I lay with my finger upon the trigger of my Henry rifle, when presently something poked its nose under the cover, and I saw at once I was surrounded by four or five lynxes, which had been attracted to my sled by the smell of provisions. Should I fire? No! That would infuriate the pack, and they would pounce upon me in a minute; so I carefully guarded every loose place, determined that, if they should commence to tear the covering, I would then do my best; and thus I lay, until the wee hours of morning, listening to their walking about my bed, and growling at each other. It certainly was not a very pleasant place to be in, and I have faint recollections of being just a little frightened.

In the morning I discovered the tracks of six animals,

and my necarnis, or best Indian friend, was considerably exercised over the danger I had been in. After a frugal breakfast, as the thermometer was thirty degrees below zero, we moved out to the place where no white man had ever trod before, but the Indian had been deceived; there was no coal there, so rather sedately we trudged along home. About noon we saw in the distance a group of Indians hurriedly making towards us, and as we were then on Indian ground we apprehended a small bit of danger, but in what shape it would come we did not know. "Hoist the American flag," I said to Porter, and he threw its waving folds over the sled, and we moved slowly along. Up came the Indians as though they would eat us all up, but we didn't scare worth a cent, as they soon saw. After rudely pushing things about, they concluded to divest us of our provisions, but Nor-go-ba-da, my best friend, simply put his finger on the trigger of his gun and told them that the American flag shielded us from all harm, besides which I was his friend, and nobody must injure a hair of my head. The Indians swung their guns from their backs, and in a moment more I expected death, but Nor-go-ba-da cooly remarked, "I have a spirit gun here which shoots eighteen times in a minute; let any man molest my schersmokerman (white man chief) and he dies." The Indians grunted, looked sullen, and went on their way.

Just as the sun was sinking to rest, we wound into a little bay or inlet, and in a few moments more were in the home of our Indian friend. The post of honor was given me, opposite the opening of the tepee—the best robe had been spread for my comfort; the women were gaudily painted, and the pot was on the fire boiling. My friend was on the right; my interpreter just back of me, two quite comely women with their children, on the left, and an old woman, the grandmother, and a young girl of about eighteen years of age, in front of us.

Soon after our entrance one of the women got up, left the tepee, returned with a big fish, unscaled and undressed, put it into the pot, stirred it up; no salt, no seasoning, except the dirt on it, to make it palatable.

"Good heavens! Porter," I said, "do they intend me to eat this dish?"

"Of course they do," he remarked.

"What, with the scales on and undressed?"

"Yes."

I simply ejaculated—"Lord," and awaited events. True enough, the head of the fish was presented to me as a mark of honor; and forgetting all my friends and all the past, and everything good, I had ever tasted in life, I gave one gulp and down went the fish's head to my great satisfaction. I felt like an immense chief, having accomplished so great a deed. But other pieces of the fish came along, and having bravely done the honor of my station and won the kind regard of my Indian friend, we exchanged bushunechees, or good-byes, and Porter and myself went out on to the broad lake, and into the pure night, and in the shimmering rays of the full moon wended our way to our camp on Vermilion lake, where the boys were rejoiced to see us, and where we were glad to clasp many friendly hands, having had a somewhat tedious but an exceedingly interesting trip.

A GENUINE INDIAN SCARE.

IT WAS a bright morning in June, 1863, warm, sultry, with nature dressed in her loveliest attire, when the commander of Camp Pope—now a member of congress—and all his subordinate officers retired to the river near by to bathe their limbs in the limpid water, and to fulfill the injunction of the scriptures—"wash and be cleaned." Coney Island, N. Y., could not have presented a more animated scene than this, with officers and men disporting in the stream, all alive with animation and fun. The quartermaster of the post with some six of his clerks were there, while a small guard was left at the stockade to give warning in case of danger. One can realize the supreme happiness of the moment when he comes to consider that these men had been cooped up in their temporary barracks for a long time, and were tired, and weary, and dirty, and now the "sounding aisles of the dim woods rang to the anthems of the free," as they laughed and sported in the warm water that enveloped their nude forms. Across the river was a dense forest of trees, and up the river on this side where the camp was located was a rise of ground gradually ascending until it reached the buildings of the soldiers' rendezvous. On went the sport; some had completed washing thoroughly, while others had half of their bodies cleaned, and resembled tattooed men in dime museums, when, all of a sudden, Le Rock, the fat half-breed, who had in charge the families of our friendly scouting Indians, located a mile or two out, was seen on a pony, dashing furiously toward us, and as he approached we observed his hat and shoes were gone, his shirt bosom was open, and his hair was flying in the wind. Down the hill he came like a whirlwind, and addressing the commander (then in the water) in a loud voice and in an excited manner exclaimed, "Indians coming! Indians coming!" As Le Rock was himself half Indian of course we had every reason to believe that his statement was true, and as the Indians were about to make their attack in the broad glare of day, we could arrive at no other conclusion than that they were in large force, and hence the stampede of our water nymphs was of the most amusing character. One of the writer's clerks seized his clothing, and only partially washed and entirely naked tripped it up the hill at the rate of 2:40, while others, fearing a fire from the woods opposite, crept behind some bushes or a few old logs and dressed themselves as well as they could. Major S. and myself hurried to the camp as fast as possible, and while he put the men in fighting order I mounted the best horse I had and, in company with one of my clerks, galloped up the hill to reconnoitre. Another messenger was sent out on a fleet horse to inform a party who had gone to Red Wood falls to fish to return with all possible speed, as there was danger ahead. Another soldier was mounted ready to go to Fort Ridgely for aid if it were deemed necessary. Presently the fishing party came in, their animals on a full gallop; the men had made all the defense they could for the attack, and we calmly awaited the approaching Indians. Major S. was everywhere animating the men, while I, with my companion, was inspecting the surrounding country with a field-glass to see if we could discover the enemy. Riding back into camp I said to Major S.:

"We have scanned the country in every direction, but we see no Indians."

"Did you look up the valley?" inquired the major.

"Yes."

"See anything?"

"No."

"Go out again; gain the highest point you can, look carefully, and return the instant you make any discovery."

Again we were off, and soon gained a high hill and looking up the valley, we saw two men on ponies. Could they be Indians? Let us watch and see. The glass showed that one was Le Rock, and the other was one of our own men whom Major S. had sent out to meet Le Rock, and learn the worst. They were talking deliberately together, and then they turned their horses' heads toward us and jogged leisurely down the valley. As they approached we saw plainly enough that Le Rock was all broken up. He looked like a man who had passed through a terrible battle. His dejected and forlorn expression would have made an excellent picture for an artist.

"Well, Le Rock," I inquired, "where are those horrible Indians?"

"Oh, Major," he replied, "me so sorry. We terribly scared in our camp; women hide; we see Indians coming; heap big lot; see Indian on the hill; on ponies—sure. But—but great big heap Indians, only hungry dogs of dead white people, chasing the game over the hills. Look just like Indians on ponies. Me much deceived. Me sorry."

And we four rode into camp, gave the major the news and all laughed heartily over this, our first Indian scare.

In the night we were somewhat alarmed by the yelling and firing of guns by the guard around our lodge, but on inquiring we found it was only caused by a mule trying to kill a young colt, and could not be driven off with clubs, and the guards had to try powder and lead before it would let loose its hold. At the same moment a woman, the owner of the mule, reached the spot and, finding they had killed the mule, commenced a mournful cry, which still more alarmed the camp; and this being near our lodges, everybody at once rushed to the spot; but, on finding out the truth, they commenced laughing and singing, and kept up their mirth till daylight.

Everything was ready at 4:30 a.m. for leaving, and on telling our landlord that we were ready to start, he at once ordered several of his young men to accompany us as far as Powder river, and he promised he would come up himself to bid us farewell, which he did; and we halted and he made a short speech to us and to his people, reminding them only of what he had said he would do the day previous. Then he shook hands with us all and cried with a loud voice, "Now all is said," and he left with the escort for his camp.

We continued our route until 12 o'clock; weather very hot, but everyone rejoicing to be once more on our homeward way.

The distance we traveled to reach the camp was about three hundred and twenty-six miles. We found the road pleasant [it was in a direct western course] over rolling prairies till we reached the dividing ridge of the Yellowstone and Missouri waters. The remainder of the road was filled with artemisia, or wormwood, which made our course unpleasant and difficult.

In twenty-seven days we traveled six hundred and seventy-two miles and reached the fort safe and sound.

Most respectfully,

P. J. DE SMET, S. J.

FORT SNELLING.

THIS is one of the oldest fortifications in the Northwest, having been established in the year 1819, and built in 1822, or sixty-two years ago. It is located on a high plateau at the junction of the Mississippi and Minnesota rivers, and overlooks one of the finest landscapes in thè West.

The first white child born in what is now known as Minnesota, was at Fort Snelling. The first white child that died in Minnesota, was at Fort Snelling. The first early settlers in what is now known as Minnesota, were here. The first three white women in this section of country, were at Fort Snelling. The first boat, the Virginia, that ascended the Mississippi river, in the year 1823, stopped at Fort Snelling. Here General Grant, after the surrender of Lee, and Mrs. Grant, were received by the officers and ladies of the fort and partook of a collation in what was known as the bastion, near headquarters building, which has since been torn down. Here the late Charles Sumner, General W. T. Sherman and the writer received an entertainment at the commanding officer's quarters, in 1854. Here have been exciting Indian treaties made. Here was designated the rendezvous of the troops for the war, and here is, even now, being expended by the government, not less than $250,000 in laying out streets, erecting excellent buildings, beautifying the land and making the old fort grounds one of the most attractive and most beautiful of any military reservation in the West. A huge bridge, costing about $125,000, now spans the

Mississippi at the fort, and the tourist who fails to visit this renowned spot and catch a view from its commanding position, or witness the troops there stationed, or learn something of its early history, loses that which he can never replace after he has returned to his Eastern home.

While stationed at the fort in the year 1863, I frequently met and conversed with two Indian prisoners —Shak-pe-dean and Medicine Bottle, two noted Sioux chiefs—who were awaiting the sentence of death for their crimes committed during the terrible Indian massacre in 1862. Among the other atrocities which it is alleged they did, was that of holding a mother, while they baked her babe in the oven of the kitchen stove. But I will not stain these pages with their deeds; suffice it to say that they were captured, tried, and condemned to be executed. The good heart of Abe Lincoln, however, shrank from signing the death warrant, but when Andrew Johnson came into power, he ordered their execution, and they were hung just outside of the walls of the fort. They belonged to the lower band of Sioux, and not to the Unka-papas tribe, headed by Sitting Bull.

INDIAN SPEECHES AND AN INDIAN COUNCIL.

PERHAPS we could not find better specimens of Indian oratory than those which follow. These speeches were delivered at a council with the good Father De Smet and the chiefs, at Powder river, in 1868:

SPEECH OF BLACK MOON.

"Listen well to what I am going to say." Addressing his people, he raised the pipe to the heavens, and pointed it to earth. Then addressing the Black Gown, he begged him to touch it with his lips, and let his hand rest on the stem. While doing so he said, "let us smoke," which was done, and passed round from us to others. Then in a loud voice he exclaimed: "The Black Gown came far to meet with us. He looks fatigued and careworn. I am glad to see him, I welcome him here with all my heart. His words are good and full of meaning and truth. He speaks well. Everything he says is the desire of my heart. But there are many sores in our bosoms to heal. Our country is desolated and impoverished by cruel war, of which beginning I claim no part. The Eastern Sioux and Cheyennes commenced it. It has been forced on us, and now when we travel over our country we frequently behold red spots, and they are not the red spots of the slaughtered buffalo, but of our fellow-comrades, or the white men. Our country was once full of game, but since the war the animals seem to detest their native homes, and

I believe it is in consequence of the human blood that they have been driven far away. Again, the whites have been cutting our country up with roads, building forts at different points and frequently and unkindly put our people in prison, and that for little or no cause. They ruin our country and cut our timber with impunity. I have always told them that I did not want remuneration for roads, nor would I sell my country, as some of my people have done. My father lived and died here and so would I. And if my white brothers did right, I don't think we should have, or ever have had, troubles. I have always liked to have goods to trade, but I cannot bear the idea to have the country filled with white men. Some are good; a great many are bad; they frequently treat us badly, and frequently have our people been shot by the travelers over the plains, while they were seeking food for their children, which the Great Father gave them and has taught it was their own. We have been cruelly treated and many times treacherously deceived, and this while under the protection of the white chief. But these things are past, and I now hope will be forgotten from this day. I will say no more, but will conclude my speaking by thanking you, the Black Gown, in the hearing of all my people for the truly welcome news that you have so kindly brought us. We will accept of your tobacco and the kind advice of our Great Father, and extend our hand in the presence of all, and the Great Spirit, as the hand of peace." And then turning to the assembly, he said, "Let the past be forgotten. Some of my young men will accompany you to the fort to accomplish this most of all others desired event." He then resumed his seat.

SPEECH OF TWO BEARS.

Friends: I heard of the coming of this good Black Gown months ago, and on arriving welcomed him to our country, east side of the Missouri, where I was born and raised. And as our country is common to all, I have come along with him, not alone to see some of my comrades with whom I once trailed the war path, but to hear you talk, to witness how you treat this, of all others, in my opinion, our truest and best friend. The whites love and respect him, and so do I and my people the Yanktonais, and I pray to the Great Spirit that I may always continue in the same sentiments. I wish you to understand fully what I say, for I mean it all. I do not come here to beg of you any favors on the strength of our relationship, but I have come here with a few of our chieftains and braves of the eastern Sioux, who represent some seven hundred lodges, to tell you that our minds are made up and we will be guided by his advice and the great men (the commissioners), sent by the President to accomplish something definite for our future welfare. I have listened with care and attention to all you have said in this, the most important council ever held in our country. I say the most important because it is foreboding of future weal or woe, and headed by the best of men, and seven of the greatest chiefs of the whites. It cannot be otherwise than tend to our future good and prosperity. I tell you on this occasion, one and all, that my mind is made up, and it shall be guided in the future by the advice of these men. I have been weary, fatigued and confused, troubled and perplexed with the various reports that I have heard from this source for the last two years. But seeing you all here, and having heard you all talk, and treat this party so kindly, I must thank one and all for your wise and brave conclusion. I shall leave you with a heart full of joy, and with hopes that you shall ever continue as friends to the whites, and that the dark cloud of war that has been hanging over us may be dispelled. I thank this good man, and raise my hand to the Great Spirit, that he may pity us and carefully guide our steps through all coming time.

RUNNING ANTELOPE'S SPEECH—UNKAPAPA.

Friends and Relations: I have heard this day with pleasure your welcome words to our true friend, who has been traveling for three months for no other purpose than to bring blessings upon our people and peace to our country, for which you all seem to feel inclined. for my part I have been listening to the words of the whites for these many years past, and particularly so since our late troubles—caused more by our neighboring bands (the Santes) than by ourselves. But now is not the time to talk about the past; it is high time to speak and act for the future. I have seen you and have been with you several times since our troubles, and have always talked as you now hear me. I had, on leaving the post, made up my mind to ask you once more to be at peace with the whites—and that is why you see me here to-day—but, as the request is not necessary—you having with your own good will seen the propriety of so doing, all that now remains for me to say is, I thank you in the name of the Great Spirit for your kind treatment and attention to the Black Gown and his party. For myself, I am one of you [he was an Unkapapa], and can candidly declare that this day's council has given me more satisfaction than I have experienced for many years. I return to our camp at the fort with a glad heart, and when I shall be with the great men our great father has sent, I shall talk as you have talked to-day; and when all our troubles are settled, which I hope soon to be, then shall I turn my eyes upon the Unkapapa camp and watch with eyes and ears that you are faithful to your promises made to-day before the Great Spirit and the flag of peace, which is now with you and will be left here to remind you of what you have said to the best friends of our race. Four Horns, Black Moon, Sitting Bull, Jane, White Gut, Bull Owl, No Neck, and all others—you this day by your good words and promises have set an example to follow for all other bands. Now look well to your young men, and often remind them of the advice and course pointed out to you by the Black Gown. With this truthful and only safe assurance to our future happiness, the men whom you will send to hear what the great men of the great father will say and do for our future good will be pleased, and for my part they shall not return displeased. I shall make peace and I trust shall never break it."

Here the council ended, and we returned to our lodge amidst shouts of songs and joy. The very earth seemed to shake with their dancing.

Father De Smet continues his narrative of this interesting council as follows: Sitting Bull then said when he first saw us with the flag his heart fluttered, but he bid it to be quiet; and now that he heard that it was the flag of peace, he felt easy and undisturbed. He then told the braves to take charge of us and to see that we had water and food, and requested them not on any circumstance to allow us to go far from the lodge, and to attend to the safety of our animals. They shook us heartily by the hand. Mr. Jalpin was called to almost every lodge in the village and was treated with great respect and kindness. [Sitting Bull's speech on this occasion is given elsewhere in the pages of this book.]

At 5:30 p.m. we commenced putting our effects in order to make an early start on the next day. The same caution and the same attention were given to all as before. After supper all the chiefs came to the lodge and passed the night with us, and all seemed pleased at the day's council.

EARLY MISSIONARY EFFORTS AMONG THE INDIANS.

THE REV. JOHN ELIOT was styled by his contemporaries, and he is known to posterity, as "the Apostle to the Indians." A truer philanthropist than he did not exist among the early New Englanders. In his day the feeling toward the Indians was not kindly. It seems as if the opinion prevailed then, which has since been embodied in the discreditable phrase, that "the only good Indian is a dead one." The Puritans pronounced the Indians children of the devil, and thought they did a service in ridding the world of as many of them as possible. Yet the conversion and civilization of the natives of America were among the professed objects for which the Puritans left England. The charter of Massachusetts granted by Charles I. contains an expression of the hope that the settlers to whom it is granted "may win and incite the natives of the country to the knowledge and obedience of the only true God and Savior of mankind and the Christian faith, which is our royal intention, and the adventurers' free profession is the principal end of this plantation." The first seal of Massachusetts represented an Indian giving utterance to the words, "Come over and help us."

John Eliot was a native of Nasing, in Essex, where he was born in 1604. Little is known about his family and his early years. It is unquestionable that he received a good education, but where or by whom is uncertain. His own words imply that his family were God-fearing persons who trained him with care. About the year 1630 he became usher in a school kept by the Rev. Thomas Hooker at Little Baddow, near Chelmsford. Hooker was one of the most popular Puritan clergymen of his time. His preaching at Chelmsford had been very effective; but his eloquent tongue was silenced by Laud, because he would not conform on certain points of ritual upon which Laud set great store. At the request of several influential members of his congregation, he took pupils, and engaged John Eliot as usher. The result was that Eliot became imbued with Hooker's opinions, and inspired with a desire to become a preacher of the gospel. Referring to his sojourn in Hooker's house, he wrote that "to this place I was called through the infinite riches of God's mercy in Christ Jesus to my poor soul; for here the Lord said unto my dead soul, *Live;* and through the grace of Christ I do live, and I shall live forever. When I came to this blessed family, I then saw, and never before, the power of godliness in its lively vigor and efficacy."

Eliot, having apparently incurred the suspicion of the ecclesiastical authorities, and finding insurmountable obstacles interposed to his following the profession of teacher, resolved to cross the Atlantic. He was one of sixty passengers in the ship "Lyon," which arrived at Boston on the 3d of November, 1631. Among the passengers were the wife, the eldest son, and other children of Governor Wintrop. The congregation of the first church of Boston earnestly desired that Eliot should become their pastor. Before leaving England he had promised to be the pastor in America of several families of Puritans, who contemplated emigrating thither, and, as they fulfilled their intention and settled at Roxbury, he kept his promise by settling there also. A year after landing at Boston he was married, his wife being a lady whose acquaintance he had made in England, and who followed him to America.

In a work published in 1654, entitled the "Wonder-working Providence of Sion's Saviour in New England," the following account is given of the founding of the church at Roxbury, of Roxbury itself, and of Eliot:

"The fifth church of Christ was gathered at Roxbury, situated between Boston and Dorchester, being well watered with cool and pleasant springs issuing forth from the rocky hills, and with small freshets watering the valleys of this fertile town, whose form is somewhat like a wedge, double-pointed, entering between the two fore-named towns, filled with a very laborious people, whose labors the Lord hath so blessed that in the room of dismal swamps and tearing bushes they have very goodly fruit trees, fruitful fields and gardens, their herd of cows, oxen, and other young cattle of that kind about three hundred and fifty, and dwelling-houses near upon one hundred and twenty. Their streets are large, and some fair houses, yet have they built their house for church assembly destitute and unbeautified with other buildings. The church of Christ here is increased to about one hundred and twenty persons. Their first teaching elder called to office is Mr. Eliot, a young man at his coming hither of a cheerful spirit, walking unblamable, of a godly conversation, apt to teach, as by his indefatigable pains, both with his own flock and the poor Indians, doth appear, whose language he learned purposely to help them to the knowledge of God in Christ, frequently preaching in their wigwams and catechising their children."

Few incidents of importance are preserved as to Eliot's life as pastor at Roxbury. The most noteworthy relates to an early stage in his career there, when he was taken to task by the rulers of Massachusetts for having improperly reflected upon their conduct. His offense consisted in censuring them in a sermon for having made peace with the Pequot Indians without consulting those among the people who were entitled to vote. Three clergymen who were appointed to "deal with him," brought him to acknowledge that he had erred in holding that the magistrates could not conclude a peace on their own authority, and he made public acknowledgment of his mistake. He was one of the clergymen who actively took part against Mrs. Anne Hutchinson. He was as uncharitable as any of his colleagues in treating that unfortunate woman, who was punished for her independence of spirit with excommunication and banishment.

In the year 1646, fifteen years after he had settled in New England, Eliot began to preach to the Indians in their own tongue. Before so doing he had spent some time in mastering their language. He learned it from a young native employed in his house, whom he describes as "a pregnant-witted young man who had been a servant in an English house, pretty well understood his own language, and had a clear pronunciation."

Irrespective of the philanthropy which prompted Eliot to render service to the Indians, there was an influence which specially moved him. While others held these Indians to be children of the devil, he firmly believed them to be descendants of the lost tribes of the house of Israel. To raise these people from their fallen and degraded state was, in his opinion, a sacred duty. He was not singular in thinking that the Indians were of Jewish descent; the same theory still finds adherents. The origin of the North American Indians is involved in as great mystery in our day as it was when Eliot lived. Anything may be conjectured about them with plausibility, because so very little is known with certainty. Yet it is no longer doubtful that these Indians were not the first or only inhabitants of the country before the advent of white men. Another race, called Mound Builders, which has long been extinct, possessed the land before the Indians, and they were either driven from it southward or exterminated. The lot of the Indians, owing to the conduct of the white men who have mastered and supplanted them, cannot, at the worst, be more deplorable than that of the Mound Builders whom these Indians subdued and succeeded.

After laboring for two years to obtain a colloquial command over the tongue spoken by the Indians of Massachusetts, Eliot considered himself qualified for preaching to them. The first Christian sermon in the Indian tongue delivered on the North American continent was delivered by Eliot at Nonantum on the 28th of October, 1646. His text was the 9th and 10th verses of the 37th chapter of Ezekiel—"Then said he unto me, Prophesy unto the wind, phrophesy, son of man, and say to the wind, Thus saith the Lord God: Come from the four winds, O breath, and breathe upon these slain, that they may live. So I prophesied as He commanded me, and the breath came into them, and they lived, and stood up upon their feet, an exceeding great army." In his sermon he explained the character of Christ, the purpose and manner of His appearance upon earth. He told them of the judgment day, when the wicked are to suffer and the good are to be rewarded. He urged them to repent of their sins as fallen children of Adam, and to pray to God and accept Christ as their Savior. He invited questions after his sermon, and he found it as difficult to return satisfactory replies as in our day Bishop Colenso did in the case of the inquiring Zulu.

After satisfying their curiosity, Eliot received their thanks. He neither spared himself nor them. His sermon lasted an hour and a quarter, and the conference three hours. As a reward for their patient attention, he distributed tobacco among the men and apples among the children. This was the beginning of a course of teaching which Eliot kept up during forty years, in addition to discharging his duties as pastor of Roxbury. He underwent many dangers as well as severe toil. What he sometimes endured, and the spirit which always animated him, can be gathered from his own words to Mr. Winslow: "I have not been dry, night or day, from the third day of the week until the sixth, but so traveled, and at night pull off my boots, wring my stockings, and on with them, and so continue. But God steps in and helps. I have considered the Word of God, II. Timothy, ii. 3, 'Endure hardship, as a good soldier of Jesus Christ.'"

One of the first fruits of his teaching was to excite a desire on the part of the Indians to have their children educated in the English fashion. A convert named Wampas brought his own son to Eliot, and three other children, of whom the youngest was four and the eldest was nine, with the request that they might be brought up by him in the fear and knowledge of God. The same Indian and two others sought and found situations in English families, with a view of being better instructed in religion. Difficulties of various kinds had to be overcome. In addition to accepting the religious faith offered to them by the English missionary, the Indians copied the English fashion of cropping their hair. This exposed them to the derision of their unconverted brethren. But they had a still harder trial to undergo. Speaking for his fellow converts, Wampas told Eliot that "on the one hand, the other Indians hate and oppose us because we pray to God; on the other, the English will not put confidence in us, and suspect that we do not really pray." Eliot admitted that such a suspicion was entertained by some of the English, adding that, for his part, he considered it groundless.

It was natural that the Powaws, or priests, should have objected to Eliot's work and have placed obstacles in his path. He had the triumph of converting one Powaw, but he found it hard to satisfy another who asked him how it happened that the English were twenty-seven years in the country before attempting to teach their religion to the Indians. The Powaw urged that if this had been done sooner much sin might have been prevented; "but now some of us are grown old in sin." All that could be said by way of defense and explanation was that the English had repented them of their neglect, as was evinced by the efforts which Eliot and others were then making. As a consequence of the adoption of Christianity, the Indians had to change many old habits and customs, and in doing so they were often perplexed. They were enjoined to renounce polygamy; but they asked which of their wives should they put away? They were told that gaming was sinful; but they asked was it permissible to repudiate debts contracted before their conversion through gaming with non-praying Indians? This last question gave Eliot great concern. He could not reply that gaming was lawful, nor would he countenance the breach of a promise. He found a way out of the dilemma by urging on the creditor that gaming was sinful, and persuading him to reduce his claim by one half; by informing the debtor that, though he had sinned by gaming, yet that he must fulfill his promise, and by inducing him to pay one half of what he owed. This compromise was adopted in all cases of the kind, but it led to the result of a winner at play counting upon receiving and the loser of paying half the amount in each case, so that the change was no real improvement.

The conversion of Cutshamakin, an Indian Sachem, was one of Eliot's triumphs. He did not find this Sachem a very meek or tractable Christian. On the contrary, the Sachem was not gratified to see the members of his tribe walking in new paths. He complained bitterly that the converts ceased to pay tribute to him as in the old time, and feared that he might eventually be left without any revenue. His complaint was diligently investigated. The Indians alleged that they had paid the accustomed tribute to their chief; that at one time he had received from them six bushels of maize, and twenty at another; that he had obtained their services in hunting for several days; that fifteen deer had been killed for him; that two acres of land had been broken and a large wigwam built for him. Eliot held that this was an ample payment for one year. He eventually learned that the Sachem's real grievance was, that the converted Indians were not so ready as the others to comply with all his orders and submit to his despotic rule.

Eliot's labors to benefit the Indians were so much appreciated in Massachusetts that, on the 26th of May, 1647, the General Court passed the following resolution:—"It is ordered that £10 be given to Mr. Eliot as a gratuity from this Court in respect of his pains in instructing the Indians in the knowledge of God, and that order be taken that the £20 per annum given by the Lady Armine for that purpose may be called for and employed accordingly." The tidings of his work crossed the sea and became the subject of deliberation in Parliament. It was held to be the duty of "the godly and well-affected" to aid the enterprise, and a resolution was passed on the 17th of March, 1647, desiring the committee on plantations to prepare an ordinance "for the encouragement and advancement of learning and piety in New England." No result followed till the 27th of July, 1649, when an ordinance to the same effect being passed, a corporation was founded for the propagation of the gospel in New England: a general collection was ordered to be made in the churches of England and Wales, and the clergymen were required to read the ordinance from their pulpits. The universities of Oxford and Cambridge issued an appeal in support of the undertaking. Though the sum placed at the disposal of the corporation was not large, yet it sufficed to establish schools for the Indians, to supply them with implements of husbandry, and to defray the cost of printing Eliot's translation of the Bible and other books into the Indian tongue.

When Charles II. became king it was feared that the corporation for propagating christianity among the Indians would share the fate of other institutions established during the commonwealth. Happily, the corporation for the propagation of the gospel found a warm supporter in Robert Boyle, through whose representations Lord Chancellor Clarendon advised the king to grant a new charter to it. Under this charter, Boyle was appointed governor, and he directed the affairs of the corporation with great zeal, earning Eliot's heartfelt gratitude.

It was Eliot's conviction that, unless the praying Indians, as the converts were always styled, lived in the European fashion there was a fear lest they should lapse from the right path. Accordingly, he planned a town where they might live together. It was called Natick, being situated on the banks of the Charles River, eighteen miles to the southeast of Boston. Natick is described as a town covering six thousand acres, wherein one hundred and forty Indians dwelt. It had three long streets, two on the north side and one on the south. A bridge, built by the Indians, spanned the river. There was a fort for their protection. Some families dwelt in wigwams; others in houses on the English model. A large building served as a place of meeting on Sundays and a school-house on week-days. It had an upper floor, in one corner of which a room was partitioned off to serve as a bedchamber for Eliot.

After the praying Indians had taken up their abode at Natick they applied to Eliot to devise a plan of municipal government for them. He had previously induced the converts to agree to the following, among other conditions :—"Powawing" and drunkenness were to be punished with a fine of 20s. for each offense; the person convicted of stealing was to restore fourfold the amount taken; the profaner of the Sabbath was to be fined 20s.; a wife-beater was to pay the same fine; while murder and monstrous crimes were to be punished with death. The converts likewise agreed to pray in their wigwams, to say grace before and after meat, to cease howling, greasing their bodies, and adorning their hair, and to follow the English fashions.

Eliot held that all governments should be founded on the pattern given in the Old Testament; he was anxious that England should set an example in this respect, holding that "it would be a blessed day in England when the word of God shall be their Magna Charta and chief law book, and when all lawyers shall be divines and study the Scriptures." It was natural, then, that he should give effect to his views at Natick, and should persuade the Indians there to divide the community into hundreds and tithings, and should appoint rulers over hundreds, rulers over fifties, and rulers over tens, or tithing men. He enjoined the payment of tithes on strictly scriptural grounds, and the Indians consented to do as he desired. Having settled the manner in which, subject to the General Court of Massachusetts, these Indians should govern themselves, Eliot induced them to enter into a solemn covenant. On the 6th of August, 1651, they assembled together, and, after divine service, the following declaration received their assent :—

"We are the sons of Adam. We and our forefathers

have a long time been lost in our sins; but now the mercy of the Lord beginneth to find us out again. Therefore, the grace of Christ helping us, we do give ourselves and our children to God, to be His people. He shall rule us in all our affairs, not only in our religion and affairs of the church, but also in all our works and affairs in this world. God shall rule over us. The Lord is our Judge; the Lord is our law-giver; the Lord is our King, He will save us. The wisdom which God hath taught us in His book, that shall guide us and direct us in the way. O Jehovah! teach us wisdom to find out thy wisdom in thy Scriptures. Let the grace of Christ help us, because Christ is the wisdom of God. Send thy Spirit into our hearts, and let it teach us. Lord, take us to be thy people, and let us take thee to be our God."

Nine years after these proceedings a further step was taken in the direction of putting the praying Indians on a footing of equality with their white brethren. A church on the congregational model was founded there, so that the Indians of Natick enjoyed the same civil and religious privileges as the Puritans of Boston. In the strict observance of their religious duties the Indians were patterns to many of their white brethren. They even complained, not without reason, that white men did not seem to be sufficiently scrupulous in their religious observances. On the other hand, the white men expected the Indians to be faultless, and regarded any error on their parts as the evidence of an ineradicably perverse nature.

The most grievous trial which the praying Indians had to endure, and the most desponding period in Eliot's dealings with them, was during the year of the war, commonly called King Philip's war, which began in 1675. This was the most vigorous effort as well as the last combined attempt of the Indians to exterminate the white men in New England. The loss of life was great on both sides; as many as six hundred of the settlers were slain. Much property was destroyed. Thirteen towns were laid in ruins; hundreds of dwellings were burned to the ground. Whilst the hostilities between the Indians and white men were in progress, the position of the praying Indians was very trying. Their brethren in race regarded them as enemies; the white men did not count them as friends. Indeed, all Indians were not only regarded as foes at heart, but every Indian's life was in danger at the hands of the exasperated and panic-stricken whites. The General Court, unable to withstand the pressure of public opinion, ordered that the Indians at Natick should be transported for safe custody to Deer Island. They quietly submitted to their fate. After the death of Philip the Indians were permitted to return, at their own expense, to their old homes. Such as did return keenly felt that the love and charity, which they had been enjoined to practice, were not displayed towards them. King Philip's war proved the hopelessness of any struggle in the field between Indians and white men, while it gave a blow to the spread of Christianity among the Indians. The latter were indisposed to listen to teachers whose brethren flagrantly violated the precepts which they inculcated.

In 1797, one hundred and twenty-one years after the war which ended with Philip's death, the Rev. Stephen Badger, minister at Natick, was asked to give an account of the Indians there. He was then in his seventy-second year, and had beheld many changes. The white men had ousted the Indians from their property and offices at Natick before the time that Mr. Badger wrote; the church members had been reduced to two or three; one of them was an aged Indian woman, who could still understand the tongue of her people, but could not speak it. At the present day not an Indian in existence can speak the language which Eliot learned in order to preach the gospel, and into which he translated the Bible. His translation of the Bible is a monument of vast labor. The only practical value of that translation now consists in the service it renders to the philological students who investigate the dead tongue of an extinct race. Besides the Bible, Eliot translated the catechism and Baxter's "Call to the Unconverted" and the "Practice of Piety." He labored zealously and without ceasing during a long life. In 1688 he wrote to Boyle, saying, "I am drawing home," and on 20th May, 1690, he pessed away, in his eighty-sixth year, uttering the words, "Welcome, joy."

Eliot's wife, whom he married the year after he settled in New England, died three years before him. He had six children, of whom a son and a daughter alone survived him. He owed much to his wife, who managed his household admirably. He was not exacting in domestic affairs, and his tastes were so simple that he was very easily pleased; he liked the plainest food, and he drank water from choice. He had two great aversions—wigs and tobacco. Wearing wigs he regarded as a lust of the flesh, and tobacco he considered a weed produced by satan for man's injury.

The blunders with which Eliot is chargeable are few and trivial, while his good deeds are innumerable. His character is without reproach; he was one of the small band of Puritans in whom there was no guile. Unhappily, he could not leave behind him a body of men imbued with his spirit and fitted to continue his work from generation to generation. Had the Indians on the North American Continent been constantly treated in the spirit which animated Eliot, the history of the United States would be free from many grievous stains. It was not Eliot's fault that the Indians of New England faded away till the land wherein they were once supreme did not contain a single survivor. His memory is still held in honor as that of one who loved his fellow-men, and who devoted a long and laborious life to their service.

INDIAN POETRY.

HE WILL COME.

E-ye-he-kta! E-ye-he-kta!
He-kta-ce; e-ye-ce-quon.
Mi-Wamdee-ska, he-he-kta;
He-kta-ce; e-ye-ce-quon,
  Mi-Wamdee-ska.

TRANSLATION.

He will come! he will come?
He will come, for he promised,
My White Eagle, he will come;
He will come, for he promised,—
  My White Eagle.

COME AGAIN.

Aké u, aké u, aké u;
Ma cântè maséca.
Aké u, aké u, aké u;
Ma cânté maséca.

TRANSLATION.

Come again, come again, come again;
  For my heart is sad.
Come again, come again, come again,
  For my heart is sad.

THE GIANTS' DANCE.

They dance to the tune of their wild "ha-ha!"
A warrior's shout and a raven's caw—
Circling the pot and the blazing fire
  To the tom-tom's bray and the rude bassoon;
Round and round to their hearts' desire,
  And ever the same wild chant and tune—
A warrior's shout and a raven's caw—
"Ha-ha, ha-ha, ha-ha-ha!"
They crouch, they leap, and their burning eyes
  Flash fierce in the light of the flaming fire,
  As fiercer and fiercer, and higher and higher
The rude, wild notes of their chant arise.
They cease, they sit, and the curling smoke
  Ascends again from their polished pipes,
  And upward curls from their swarthy lips
To the god whose favor their hearts invoke.

NEVER! NEVER!

My father! my father! her words were true;
And the death of Wiwâstè will rest on you.
You have pledged me as wife to the tall Red Cloud;
You will take the gift of the warrior proud;
But I, Wakâwa, I answer—never!
  I will stain your knife in my heart's red blood,
I will plunge and sink in the sullen river,
  Ere I will be wife to the fierce Red Cloud.

GRANDFATHER.

Tunkânsidân pejihúta wakán
Micâgè—he wicâgè
Mimyáta ité wakándé makú
Tankánsidan ite, nâpè dú-win-ta-woo,
Wahutôpa wan yúha, nápè du-win-ta-too.

TRANSLATION.

Grandfather made me magical medicine;
That is true!
Being of mystery—grown in the water—
He gave it me!
To the face of our Grandfather stretch out your hand;
Holding a quadruped, stretch out your hand!

TO THE SPIRIT LAND.

At last, when their locks were as white as snow,
Beloved and honored by all the band,
They silently slipped from their lodge below,
And walked together, and, hand-in-hand,
O'er the shining path to the spirit land.